Tomorrow's Geography
for Edexcel GCSE Specification A
REVISION GUIDE

UNIT 3 The Human Environment

Mike Harcourt
Steph Warren

HODDER
EDUCATION
AN HACHETTE UK COMPANY

The Publishers would like to thank the following for permission to reproduce copyright material:

Photo credits: **page 2** *l* © Imagestate Media, *c* © gerenme/iStockphoto.com, *r* © Corbis. All Rights Reserved; **page 6** *l* © Imagestate Media, *r* © Ingram Publishing Ltd.; **page 25** © Steph Warren; **page 26** © Steph Warren; **page 29** © JORGEN SCHYTTE/Still Pictures; **page 39** *t*, *b* © Mike Harcourt; **page 49** *l*, *r* © Mike Harcourt; **page 53** *l*, *r* © Steph Warren; **page 58** *t*, *b* © Steph Warren; **page 59** © Steph Warren.

Every effort has been made to trace all copyright holders, but if any have been inadvertently overlooked the Publishers will be pleased to make the necessary arrangements at the first opportunity.

Although every effort has been made to ensure that website addresses are correct at time of going to press, Hodder Education cannot be held responsible for the content of any website mentioned in this book. It is sometimes possible to find a relocated web page by typing in the address of the home page for a website in the URL window of your browser.

Hachette UK's policy is to use papers that are natural, renewable and recyclable products and made from wood grown in sustainable forests. The logging and manufacturing processes are expected to conform to the environmental regulations of the country of origin.

Orders: please contact Bookpoint Ltd, 130 Milton Park, Abingdon, Oxon OX14 4SB. Telephone: (44) 01235 827720. Fax: (44) 01235 400454. Lines are open 9.00–5.00, Monday to Saturday, with a 24-hour message answering service. Visit our website at www.hoddereducation.co.uk

© Mike Harcourt and Steph Warren

First published in 2003 by
Hodder Education,
An Hachette UK Company
338 Euston Road
London NW1 3BH

This second edition published in 2010.

Impression number   5 4 3 2 1
Year   2014 2013 2012 2011 2010

All rights reserved. Apart from any use permitted under UK copyright law, no part of this publication may be reproduced or transmitted in any form or by any means, electronic or mechanical, including photocopying and recording, or held within any information storage and retrieval system, without permission in writing from the publisher or under licence from the Copyright Licensing Agency Limited. Further details of such licences (for reprographic reproduction) may be obtained from the Copyright Licensing Agency Limited, Saffron House, 6–10 Kirby Street, London EC1N 8TS.

Illustrations by Gray Publishing
Produced and typeset in 11/13pt Myriad by Gray Publishing, Tunbridge Wells
Printed in Italy

A catalogue record for this title is available from the British Library

ISBN: 978 1444 11534 5

Contents

Unit 3 The Human Environment

Chapter 1 Economic Change — 2
- Changes to different economic sectors — 2
- Economic locations — 7

Chapter 2 Farming and the Countryside — 9
- Changes to the UK countryside — 9
- Management of the UK countryside — 16

Chapter 3 Settlement Change — 20
- Factors affecting settlements — 20
- Changing land use in urban areas — 24
- Rapid growth in LICs — 28

Chapter 4 Population Change — 30
- Population growth and distribution — 30
- Characteristics of population — 37

Chapter 5 A Moving World — 41
- Population movement — 41
- Flows of population — 42
- Factors enabling population movement — 44
- Reasons for short-term population flows — 46
- Retirement migration — 49

Chapter 6 A Tourist's World — 52
- Growth of the tourist industry — 52
- Resort development — 54
- The effects of tourist industry growth — 55
- Ecotourism — 60

1 Economic Change

Changes to different economic sectors

What are the sectors of industry?

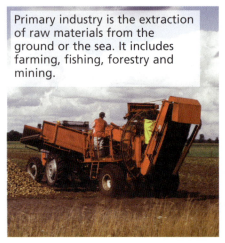

Primary industry is the extraction of raw materials from the ground or the sea. It includes farming, fishing, forestry and mining.

Secondary industry is the manufacturing of goods using the raw materials from primary industry, for example paper-making processes the raw material of wood to produce paper.

Tertiary industry does not produce anything, but often involves the provision of different services. Teachers, solicitors, sales assistants and cleaners are all tertiary occupations.

Figure 1 Three categories of industry

How do employment patterns differ between countries?

The relative importance of primary, secondary and tertiary industries can be used to compare the levels of development between countries. The following pie charts show the percentage of the population working in the three sectors of industry. The charts are for Germany (HIC), Taiwan (MIC) and Mali (LIC).

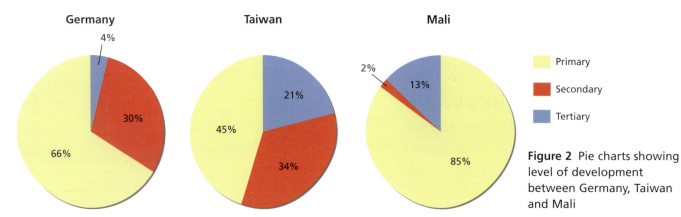

Figure 2 Pie charts showing level of development between Germany, Taiwan and Mali

- Mali has a high proportion of the population working in primary industries, mostly farming. This is very common in LICs.
- A high proportion of the workforce of an HIC such as Germany is involved in the tertiary sector. Up to 70% of the workforce in some HICs with mature economies are in tertiary occupations.
- Taiwan is an MIC and has a strong secondary sector. Many transnational companies have factories in countries like Taiwan so that they can take advantage of cheaper labour and land. These countries are transitional between HICs and LICs and so still have a large farming population and a growing tertiary sector.

ACTIVITY

How can you use employment patterns to determine if a country is an HIC, MIC or LIC?

Chapter 1 Economic Change

How do employment patterns change over time?

In the UK three trends have occurred in the past 150 years.
1. A steady decrease in the primary sector that has been caused by:
   - Improvements in technology, which led to increased mechanisation. This has reduced the need for agricultural workers.
   - Many raw materials, for example iron ore and coal, have been used up or are cheaper to import from abroad.
   - Jobs in primary industries are often seen to be 'dirty' and to have few career prospects. Workers prefer the better paid and less physically demanding jobs in the tertiary sector.
2. An increase in tertiary employment.
   - This was gradual but steady until the Second World War, then this was slightly reversed due to increased manufacturing as part of the war effort.
   - The growth in the tertiary sector increased rapidly in the final decades of the twentieth century. Most of this was in the new hi-tech industries, such as micro-electronics, and in associated fields like research and development.
3. The manufacturing industries were steady until the 1950s, then they started to decline with the decline becoming more pronounced in the 1990s.
   - The decline was due to the cheaper labour in LICs which encouraged manufacturing industries to locate there.

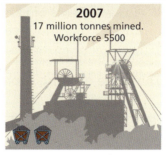

Figure 3 The declining coal mining industry as shown by the number of trucks on each diagram. One truck represents roughly 10 million tonnes of coal mined.

What are the reasons for the decline in numbers employed in the primary sector in the UK?

1 Depletion of resources
The mining industry has declined because many raw materials which used to be mined in the UK have been used up. Figure 3 shows how coal mining has declined in the UK.

2 Cheap imports
It has become cheaper to import raw materials from abroad; the Port Talbot steel works in South Wales gets its iron ore from Norway and its coal from Russia. The raw materials that remain in the UK are difficult to mine as they are deep underground.

3 Mechanisation
Mechanisation has reduced the need for the number of workers in primary industry.
- Agricultural machinery has over the past 30 years got progressively larger. It is now possible for one worker and a combine harvester to do in one day what 20 workers used to do in a week.
- Chickens and other animals are reared in factory conditions where they are automatically fed and given water.
- Fishing vessels have become much larger and more efficient with electronic equipment used to locate fish shoals and automatic fishing nets.
- Specialised machinery can dig vast amounts of coal quickly from the seams.

4 Social change
- Jobs in primary industry are often seen to be 'dirty' and hard work.
- There are fewer career prospects in the primary sector.
- Primary jobs are often low paid.
- Tertiary sector jobs also tend to have more regular hours.

Exam Tip

For questions that ask for examples, your answer will be marked as follows:

Foundation Tier – Each point will receive a mark. If your answer does not contain a specific point about an example, you will lose one mark.

Higher Tier – If the command word is **outline** or **describe**, these questions will usually be marked out of four marks. Each point will receive a mark. If your answer does not include specific points about an example, you will only receive two marks. If examples are asked for and you only give one you will lose one mark.

Unit 3 The Human Environment

What are the reasons for the decline in the secondary sector in the UK?

1 Cheaper production in LICs and MICs

Factories are closing in the UK because goods are being made cheaper in LICs and MICs. Why?
- Land and labour are cheaper.
- There are fewer regulations about health and safety so money does not have to be spent on personal protection or employing safety officers.
- Governments of LICs are not so worried about environmental impacts so money does not need to be spent on waste disposal and reprocessing.

2 Globalisation

This is the growing economic interdependency of countries worldwide.

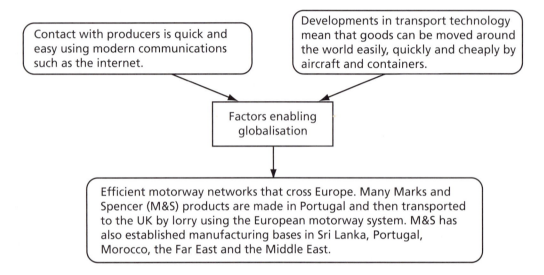

What are the reasons for the growth of the secondary sector in China?

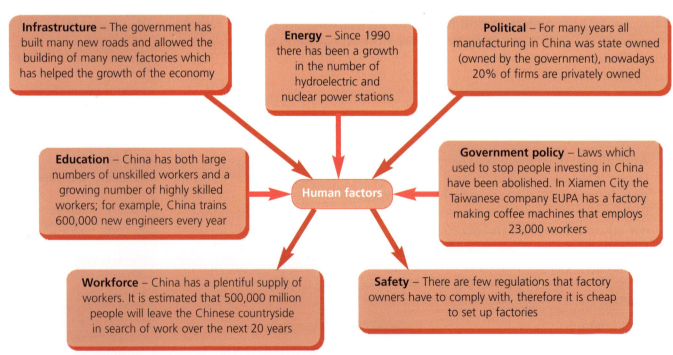

Figure 4 The human factors affecting growth of the secondary sector in China

Chapter 1 Economic Change

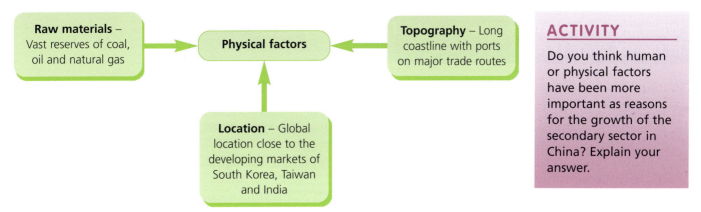

Figure 5 The physical factors affecting growth of the secondary sector in China

ACTIVITY

Do you think human or physical factors have been more important as reasons for the growth of the secondary sector in China? Explain your answer.

The effects of the growth of the secondary sector in China

The effects have been positive and negative.

Economic	Social	Environmental
Rising incomes and higher standard of living for many urban people.	Improved urban housing.	$172 billion spent by the government on environmental protection.
A growth in the economy – world's second largest manufacturing country and fourth largest economy.	Money is being invested in education. At the moment there is often only one teacher for every 80 students.	Renewable energy will increase by 16% by 2016.
Exports are greater than imports.	Few laws to protect workers who are forced to work long hours.	Damaging the environment by mining for raw materials to power the industrial growth.
Widening gap between rich and poor.	Large numbers of rural workers are moving to the urban areas for factory jobs.	Heavy pollution from burning coal which is used to power the factories. Linfen is most heavily polluted city in the world with three million people being affected.
Poor pay for the factory workers – only 40p per hour.	Government spending on health is less than in 1980.	760,000 deaths a year through air and water pollution. 80% of rivers are polluted.

Exam Tip

- You could be asked questions that require recall of knowledge. You should learn specific positive and negative points for social, economic and environmental.
- Read the question carefully and don't get caught out.

5

Unit 3 The Human Environment

What are the reasons for the growth of the tertiary sector in the UK since 1970?

1 A rise in demand for services linked to disposable incomes

- Disposable income is the amount of money that an individual has available to spend on non-essential items after essential bills have been met. Households on average are getting richer.
- The average amount that households had to spend on non-essential items doubled between 1987 and 2006.
- This meant that there was a rise in luxury services such as beauticians and health clubs. In 2000, four million people were members of fitness centres. This has continued to rise by 12% a year.

2 The development of new technologies

- Technology has created jobs in new services such as computing and telecommunications.
- Most high streets now have a number of shops that sell mobile phones, service and sell laptops and PCs, and provide photocopying facilities. There is also the development of communications such as the internet.
- Many people now shop and bank on the internet. This has caused the development of many jobs to service the websites.
- Large numbers of people are employed at call centres; 950,000 employed in 2008.

3 Decrease in employment in the primary and secondary sectors

- The decrease in the employment in the primary and secondary sectors means there must be an increase in the tertiary sector.

4 Demographic changes

People in their twenties and thirties

The ageing population

> **ACTIVITY**
>
> Explain the demographic factors that have caused a growth in the tertiary sector.

> I spend a high proportion of my income on entertainment and socialising. I go to the beautician all the time to have my nails done. There are so many coffee shops and bars on the high street. We have no children so have no ties and plenty of disposable income to spend.

> I go on holiday with Saga because there are a lot of people my age. We have money and time for holidays. I go to the gym three times a week. I spend some of my 'grey pounds' on gardening. I visit the garden centre frequently. I'm buying my Christmas presents on the internet. When I get home I will surf on the 'Saga Zone'.

Chapter 1 Economic Change

Economic locations

What factors affect the location of primary industry?

China clay (kaolin) extraction, St Austell, Cornwall

- Kaolin is only found in the south-west of England.
- There was a demand for china clay for the production of porcelain. The pottery manufacturer Josiah Wedgwood based in Stoke-on-Trent formed the Cornish clay company. This ensured the success of the industry as the mined kaolin had a definite market. By 1860, 65,000 tons was being mined each year, much of it for the Wedgwood factory in Stoke-on-Trent.
- The china clay was moved by tramway and train to the ports of Charlestown, Pentewan and Par on the south coast of Cornwall. Ships then took the raw material to Liverpool where it was then transported by barge along the Trent and Mersey canal to Winsford in Cheshire and then by packhorse the final 30 miles to Stoke-on-Trent. This ensured that the china clay could be transported to the factory where it was made into the finished product, porcelain.

ACTIVITY

In the china clay example, the descriptions are coloured blue and the explanations are in red. For the examples given in the secondary and tertiary industries, underline the descriptive and explanatory points in two different colours.

Exam Tip

- You may be asked to describe a distribution on a map such as the distribution of different types of industry. You should start with general points.
- Your answer should then become more specific.
- If data is asked for, you will lose a mark if you don't include it.
- If data is not requested you should still include some as you will be given credit.

What factors affect the location of secondary industry?

Toyota car factory at Burnaston, near Derby

- The area has a tradition in car manufacturing, there are many suppliers of component parts and engineering components.
- Located on the edge of the city, it is a greenfield site with 280 hectares of flat land giving room for expansion.
- The Peak District National Park, which is close by, has many opportunities for leisure activities so workers are attracted to the area.
- Excellent transport routes. On the junction of two main trunk roads, the A50 and A38. The A50 and A38 are dual carriageways and link to the M1 and M6. This allows easy transportation of parts and the finished product throughout the UK.
- Attractive village location such as Findern for managerial workers.

What factors affect the location of tertiary industry?

David Lloyd Health Club, Hatfield

- Attractive landscaped area to attract workers.
- Next to a large indoor shopping area, The Galleria. People can shop and go to the club with just one journey.
- Salisbury village is a large area of mixed accommodation with executive and middle-class housing and modern flats for young single people who account for a high proportion of the club's clients.
- Excellent transport system – very close to junctions 3 and 4 of the A1(M), a motorway, giving easy access to a large number of potential users.
- Within walking distance of Hertfordshire University. A potential source of clients.
- Located on Hatfield business park with many large firms like T-Mobile and Ocado. Workers from these businesses will use the health club because of its proximity.

Unit 3 The Human Environment

Case study questions will use the following mark scheme:

Foundation Tier
Level 1 (1–2) A simple answer which has very little description. Could be about anywhere, not linked to any particular study.
Level 2 (3–4) A basic answer with level two being reached by there being descriptive points or a specific point or possibly a weak explanation. The top of the level requires a specific point and some linked descriptive points or a specific point and weak explanation.
Level 3 (5–6) A clear answer with level three being reached by there being a clear explanation or a specific point. The top of the level requires a range of specific points or a number of explanations or a specific point and an explanation.

Higher Tier
Level 1 (1–2) A basic answer which has simple descriptive statements.
Level 2 (3–4) A clear answer with level two being reached by there being an explanation or a specific point. The top of the level requires a range of specific points or a number of explanations or a specific point and an explanation.
Level 3 (5–6) An explicit answer with a range of specific and explained points.

What are the benefits and costs of deindustrialisation in rural areas?

Deindustrialisation means that rural areas are no longer used for industrial purposes

Benefits of deindustrialisation	Costs of deindustrialisation
Old industrial buildings are turned into tourist attractions, for example the Eden Project in Cornwall redeveloped a disused china clay pit.	There are job losses in the countryside.
Less environmental pollution caused by factory outputs.	Rural communities have been broken up as people move to urban areas for work.
Reagriculturalisation in which land is returned to farming (Bays Leap farm).	Many ugly buildings and disused quarries remain to scar the landscape.
New wildlife habitats are created.	It has cost local authorities a lot of money to clean up derelict areas.
New forestry areas can be created such as The National Forest on old coal deposits between Burton on Trent and Swadlincote.	
Old, ugly industrial buildings can be demolished.	
Recreation areas can be made such as the Cotswold water park converted from old gravel workings and the Madejski stadium on the edge of Reading.	

ACTIVITY
Research on the internet or think back to the case studies you have discussed in class to find examples of the costs of deindustrialisation.

2 Farming and the Countryside

Changes to the UK countryside

What changes are occurring in the UK countryside and what are the consequences of these changes?

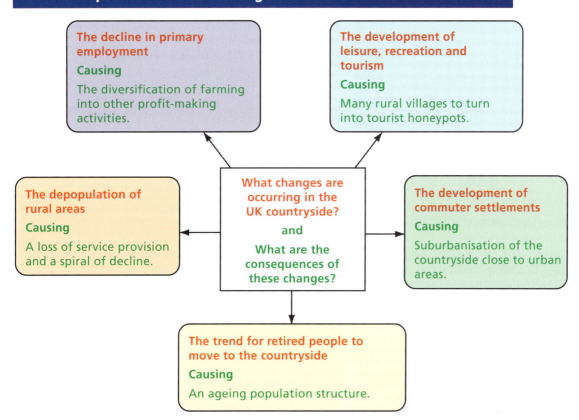

A decline in primary employment
Primary industry involves extracting raw materials from the land or the sea. It includes farming, fishing, forestry and mining.

In the UK there has been a decline in the number of people employed in the primary industry over the past 60 years.

- The number of people employed in coal mining fell from nearly 600,000 in 1960 to 10,000 in 1995.
- In 1990, 600,000 were employed in farming, by 2007 the number had declined to 500,000.

The reason for the decline in primary industry is a reduction in the need for workers due to increased mechanisation. There has been a reduction in the number employed in farming because of the nature of the work. The work involves long hours for little pay which puts people off plus the fact that there are few career prospects.

There has been a reduction in workers in the extraction (mining) industries due to the availability of cheap imports.

One consequence of this decline is the diversification of farming into other profit-making activities
British farmers have had to diversify their buildings and land in order to survive. In 2005, farmers earned 23% less for the food they produced than in 1988. Due to this they have had to diversify.

- Some farmers have turned their sheds into commercial units providing space and security for small firms. For example, in Elms Farm one of the units is occupied by 'Simply Wrought' who make wrought-iron gates and signs.
- Other farmers have used their original business but have developed into manufacturing their own products and selling them to supermarkets. For example, the Keebles who were pig farmers in Yorkshire with 350 sows, were faced with going out of business in 1999 due to cheap pork imports. They started to make their own bacon and sausages; they stressed the personal touch in their marketing and now have a turnover of £2 million.

Unit 3 The Human Environment

The depopulation of rural areas

The decline in primary employment in rural areas has led to rural depopulation. This is the movement out of rural areas by people either looking for better employment opportunities or for a better provision of facilities.

- The 2001 census states that only 24% of the in-migrants to rural areas are aged 16–29 compared with 33% of the out-migrants.
- As the population has become wealthier, there has been a demand for the provision of leisure activities both after work and at the weekend. While a rural area can provide this for some people, it is limited in what it can provide for young adults. Therefore as employment has declined and better facilities have become available in urban areas, people have moved away from rural areas.

This has left rural areas such as Cornwall with an ageing population. The population pyramid for Cornwall shows 34% of the population is over 65. When the whole of the UK is considered, 18% of people who live in rural areas are 65 or over.

The loss of service provision and a spiral of decline

This movement of people out of rural areas has caused a spiral of decline. This means that as there are fewer people using the services such as village shops, they have to close, which then causes more people to move away from the village. Other services which have closed have been village schools.

- In Cornwall, 34 village primary schools may have to close because they do not have enough children attending them.
- When the government recently announced that many Post Offices in the UK were to be closed, 50 of them were in Cornwall.

The trend for retired people to move to the countryside causing an ageing population structure

When some people retire, they want to move away from the noise and stress of living in an urban area and move to a more tranquil location. This might be in a small rural village or in a town in a more rural area. Large numbers of people have moved to the south-west of England which has a slower pace of life and milder climate than the south-east where many of them have moved from. In Cornwall, 34% of the population is over 65. The average for the UK is 25%.

Another area that people retire to is North Norfolk. But why do people retire to North Norfolk?

- Property market – the average house price in 2008 in East Anglia was approximately £200,000, whereas in greater London which supplies a high proportion of the migrants it was over £335,000.
- Scenery – the natural beauty and landscape of North Norfolk is one of its attractions. Much of the area lies within the North Norfolk Area of Outstanding Natural Beauty (AONB) and the coastline is a designated Heritage Coast.
- Climate – Norfolk is one of the driest counties in England with warm summers and an average annual rainfall of only 625 mm.
- Lifestyle – many people who retire to North Norfolk are attracted by the slower pace of life that is found in rural areas. They are also attracted by lower crime rates, particularly the low number of violent crimes. Between April 2005 and March 2006, 330 fewer offences of violence were reported.

The development of commuter settlements leading to the suburbanisation of the countryside close to urban areas

Commuters are people who live in smaller settlements close to urban areas. They wish to live in a rural environment and yet still have the benefits of the wider employment choice of a large urban area and the benefits it can offer in the way of entertainment, education, etc. One such commuter settlement is the village of Austrey in Warwickshire. Austrey began to grow in the 1970s when many new housing estates were built in the village, usually on adjacent farmland. More recently the development has been the conversion of old farm buildings into homes.

- Population in 1961: 300 with 18 working farms.
- Population in 2001: 1000 with two working farms.
- St Nicholas Close and Elms Drive built in 1960s with 25 houses on each estate.
- Bishops Cleeve built on farmland and the site of the village social club in the 1980s.
- In 1961 the village school had 16 children on roll. By 1970 there were 100 children on roll.

Chapter 2 Farming and the Countryside

The development of leisure, recreation and tourism

The countryside has also seen the development of the leisure and recreation industry. This is possibly the most obvious change as the countryside has diversified to survive.

In 1997, rural tourism generated £12 billion in consumer spending and supported 380,000 jobs either directly or indirectly. Recreation and tourism in rural areas is now a larger employer and generates more income than farming. These benefits are not equally distributed: some areas of the country, although offering attractions, are not so well known. It is the north-west and the south-west of the UK which benefit but also suffer the most from recreation and tourism. There is also a problem with seasonality and there is a need to develop out-of-season attractions.

Many rural villages have turned into tourist honeypots

One village that has benefited and lost from tourism is Malham in Yorkshire. There is very little left of the original farming village. The services in the village have been developed for tourism and most of the villagers are employed in the tourist industry.

- The local shop stays open all week in the summer due to the trade from tourists. In the winter it is only open three days a week.
- There are a large number of billboards, such as the Yorkshire Dales pony trekking centre board, displayed in the main street even though the National Park authority has banned them because they ruin the authenticity of the village.
- There are also numerous cafés and shops in the village which cater for the tourists, such as the Cove Centre. These provide employment opportunities for the local people.
- The farmer at Town Head Farm has opened a campsite charging £10 a night per tent.
- Tourism provides new jobs such as a waitress at the Barn Tea Shop. The employment is, however, seasonal and poorly paid.
- Over 55% of the houses in Malham are used for holiday purposes. This makes it very difficult for the locals, especially young couples, to buy property in the area.
- The Malham area is very popular with approximately 100,000 visits per year. This causes erosion of footpaths, especially the footpath to Janet's Foss waterfall which is one of the closest attractions to the village.

ACTIVITIES

1 Define the following terms:
   - Commuter
   - Depopulation
   - Ageing population
   - Honeypot
   - Suburbanisation
   - Spiral of decline
   - Diversification.
2 Outline two changes to the UK countryside and the consequences of these changes. Use examples in your answer.

Exam Tip

For questions that ask for examples, your answer will be marked as follows:

Foundation Tier – Each point will receive a mark. If your answer does not contain a specific point about an example you will lose one mark.

Higher Tier – If the command word is **outline** or **describe**, these questions will usually be marked out of four marks. Each point will receive a mark. If your answer does not include specific points about an example, you will only receive two marks. If examples are asked for and you only give one, you will lose one mark.

Unit 3 The Human Environment

A UK farm that has diversified – Home Farm, Hampton in Arden

Home Farm in Hampton in Arden is owned and farmed by Mr Redfern. During the past 10 years Mr Redfern has begun to diversify his farm. This is due to the decrease in subsidies for arable crops which meant that his income from crops decreased by £40,000 between 1998 and 1999, with a further decrease in 2000. The farm has only made a profit on its arable crops in 2 of the past 6 years.

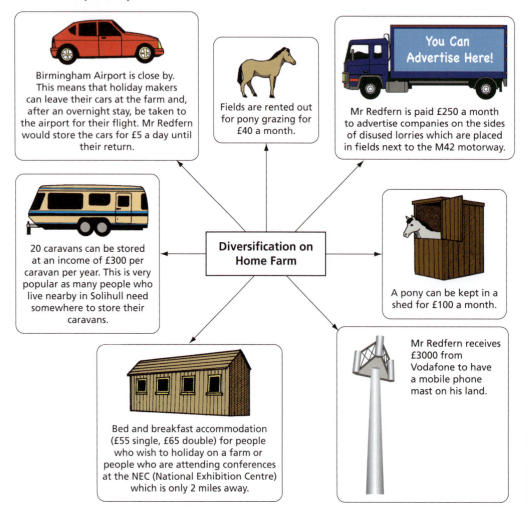

Birmingham Airport is close by. This means that holiday makers can leave their cars at the farm and, after an overnight stay, be taken to the airport for their flight. Mr Redfern would store the cars for £5 a day until their return.

Fields are rented out for pony grazing for £40 a month.

Mr Redfern is paid £250 a month to advertise companies on the sides of disused lorries which are placed in fields next to the M42 motorway.

20 caravans can be stored at an income of £300 per caravan per year. This is very popular as many people who live nearby in Solihull need somewhere to store their caravans.

Diversification on Home Farm

A pony can be kept in a shed for £100 a month.

Bed and breakfast accommodation (£55 single, £65 double) for people who wish to holiday on a farm or people who are attending conferences at the NEC (National Exhibition Centre) which is only 2 miles away.

Mr Redfern receives £3000 from Vodafone to have a mobile phone mast on his land.

ACTIVITY

Explain the ways that Mr Redfern has diversified his farm.

Exam Tip

Case study questions will use the following mark scheme:

Foundation Tier
Level 1 (1–2) A simple answer which has very little description. Could be about anywhere, not linked to any particular study.
Level 2 (3–4) A basic answer with level two being reached by there being descriptive points or a specific point or possibly a weak explanation. The top of the level requires a specific point and some linked descriptive points or a specific point and weak explanation.
Level 3 (5–6) A clear answer with level three being reached by there being a clear explanation or a specific point. The top of the level requires a range of specific points or a number of explanations or a specific point and an explanation.

Higher Tier
Level 1 (1–2) A basic answer which has simple descriptive statements.
Level 2 (3–4) A clear answer with level two being reached by there being an explanation or a specific point. The top of the level requires a range of specific points or a number of explanations or a specific point and an explanation.
Level 3 (5–6) An explicit answer with a range of specific and explained points.

Chapter 2 Farming and the Countryside

What changes have there been to UK farming practice in the twenty-first century?

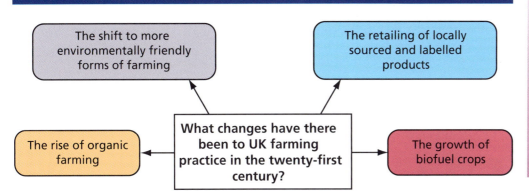

ACTIVITIES
1 How do farmers earn money by farming in a more environmentally friendly way?
2 What is organic farming?
3 Why do some people prefer organically grown products?

The shift to more environmentally friendly forms of farming

Farmers now only receive money from the EU if they are farming in an environmentally friendly way. The scheme is called the Environmental Stewardship Scheme. Farmers enter into a 5-year agreement to protect a certain amount of their land. There are a range of 50 options they can choose from and each of the options earns the farmer points:
- hedgerow management (22 points per 100 m)
- beetle banks (580 points per hectare)
- stone wall management (15 points per 100 m)
- buffer strips (300 points per hectare).

Farmers must register 30 points a hectare for them to receive £30 a hectare. They will receive this for each year of the scheme. Farmers have to submit a plan of what they are going to do which is then checked annually by Defra.

There are now over 4 million hectares of land being farmed in the scheme in a more environmentally friendly way.

Advantages	Disadvantages
The increase in wildlife in countryside areas. For example, in Devon the numbers of hedgerow birds has increased. The number of pairs of cirl buntings had decreased to only 118 pairs in 1989; 450 pairs were recorded in 2007.	Farmers have to fill in lots of paperwork and have the inconvenience of people inspecting their efforts.
Farmers receive money for working with nature rather than against it.	Farmers do not feel that they are really farming because they are not using the land to its maximum potential.

The rise of organic farming

Organic farming is growing crops and rearing animals without the use of chemicals. In 2002, 740,000 hectares of land were farmed organically compared to 50,000 hectares in 1998. During 2006 the sales from box schemes, farmers' markets and farm shop sales grew by 54% and is now worth approximately £150 million. Sales of organic food in supermarkets rose 21% in the same time period.

There are a number of reasons for this, including:
- organic food is no longer bought by just the middle classes; over 50% of people in lower income groups are now buying organic produce and this is where the market increase has come from
- three-quarters of parents now buy organic baby food
- many school dinners are now being sourced from organic farms
- more farmers' markets are being organised
- box schemes are taking off due to the internet.

Advantages	Disadvantages
Organic farming provides 30% more jobs than non-organic.	Crop yields are lower, therefore more land is needed for the same output.
Better for animals because they are kept in free-range conditions.	Organically reared cattle burp twice as much methane as conventionally reared cattle.
30% more wild species of plants and animals.	A hectare of non-organic farmed land produces 2.5 times more potatoes than organic.
36% lower incidence of eczema in children who have organic dairy products.	According to some sources, a litre of organic milk requires 80% more land than conventional milk to produce, and contributes 20% more to global warming.
Produce is pesticide- and insecticide-free, it contains more vitamin C and essential minerals such as calcium and iron.	

13

Unit 3 The Human Environment

The retailing of locally sourced and labelled products
Between 2000 and 2006, Natural England ran a campaign with the slogan 'Eat the View' which promoted the sourcing of foods locally. If foodstuffs are sourced locally it will reduce their carbon footprint. Many people are now aware of the impact of importing food from other countries due to the carbon emissions this causes and are willing to pay a little extra to buy food that has been produced locally. Large supermarkets are now sourcing many of their foods locally.

ACTIVITY
What does retailing of locally sourced products mean? Use examples in your answer.

Asda has 500 local suppliers, many of whom have fewer than 20 employees.

Somerfield, in the south-west of England, sources all of its beef locally and has contracts with 1500 farmers to supply cattle for 140 Somerfield shops in the area. For example, one farmer in Dorset supplies three cattle every week of the year to Somerfield.

Tesco buys much of its products locally, for example, Adnams beer is brewed in East Anglia and sold at local Tesco stores. Much of Tesco's meat comes from British farms, for example, 90% of fresh chicken and 95% of its beef.

Waitrose has opened 100 new food stores in market towns. The shops will be individual and will sell 200% more local products than its larger stores.

Advantages	Disadvantages
Carbon footprint of products is less.	Food can be more expensive.
Jobs are provided for local people on farms and in food packaging.	Only products in season can be supplied locally, for example strawberries would have a restricted growing season.
More money is coming into the local community.	There is not such a wide range of products available.
Monitoring of farms can be more rigorous.	

Chapter 2 Farming and the Countryside

The growth of biofuel crops

These are crops which are grown to produce energy. They include:
- Short rotation coppice of willow and poplar which can be harvested after 3 years.
- Micanthus (elephant grass) which is a grass from Asia. Once planted it can grow up to 3.5 m high and can be harvested annually for 15 years.

Others such as wheat and sugar beet can be converted into bioethanol.

To encourage the growth of biofuels, the government introduced the energy crops scheme. This led to the planting of 4500 hectares of energy crops before 2007 and a further 8600 were approved in 2006 for planting in 2007.

Under the new scheme, £47 million is available to support the establishment of 60,000 hectares of energy crops. A grant will be paid amounting to 40% of the costs to grow and harvest the crops. Crops should only be moved a maximum of 40 km before being processed into their end use.

Advantages	Disadvantages
They are biodegradable.	The grain required to fill the petrol tank of a Range Rover with ethanol is sufficient to feed one person per year.
They contain no sulphur, the element responsible for acid rain.	A land area twice the size of Britain is needed to get enough biofuel crops to halve our greenhouse gas emissions.
Vehicle engines last longer when using it.	37 countries across the world are facing food shortages.
Using biofuels could help the UK reach its target under the Kyoto Protocol to reduce its greenhouse gas emissions by 12.5% below 1990 levels by 2008–12.	The global food price index rose by 40% in 2008 to the highest level on record.
On average, biofuels produce 78% less carbon dioxide than fossil fuels.	Scrapping of set-a-side for growth of biofuels will cause problems for birds, insects and biodiversity.

ACTIVITIES

1. What are biofuels?
2. Why is there controversy over the growing of these crops?

Exam Tip

Learn details about the change and some specific advantages and disadvantages for each of the following changes:
- The shift to more environmentally friendly forms of farming.
- The rise of organic farming.
- The growth of biofuel crops.
- The retailing of locally sourced and labelled products.

Unit 3 The Human Environment

Management of the UK countryside

Management body	Reason for designation	Management
World Heritage sites.	They are areas of outstanding universal value which will disappear if not protected. They are in two categories: • a type of building with cultural importance • a natural feature which is unique from an aesthetic or scientific point of view.	• The UK government is responsible for the sites. • The local authority or other owner of the land must ensure that the sites are protected. • Management plans are prepared for each of the sites and usually last for 5 years.
National Parks.	They are areas of land which have outstanding value in terms of their natural beauty, environment or recreational value. The designation as a National Park gives the area special protection and means that resources are available to promote and manage tourism in the area.	• Each of the National Parks have their own National Park Authority. • Management plan to last for 5–10 years. • People employed to manage the park including wardens to ensure that the plan is carried out. • Special funds are available to landowners and certain restrictions apply on development.
Country Parks.	To provide an area for recreation and leisure opportunities close to population centres. They do not necessarily have any nature conservation. 　To be designated a Country Park, an area must have a number of different criteria such as: toilets on site or nearby, a daily staff presence, an up-to-date management plan and a size of at least 10 hectares (25 acres).	• They are managed by the local authority. • All parks have a management plan. • Each Country Park has a site manager and a number of estate workers who are paid to look after the site.
National Nature Reserves (NNRs).	They are usually designated for their broad ecological value and not the presence of a particular species, although some do have a particular species to be protected. Recreation is now becoming a part of their role.	• Natural England may buy the land. • The land may be in private ownership but the owners may have a nature reserve agreement with Natural England. • The land is owned by an 'approved body', for example the Wildlife Trust. • Each NNR has a site manager and a number of estate workers who are paid to look after the site. • Each site has a management plan which usually lasts for 5 years. • The majority of NNRs allow the public some access. School groups and students are given educational tours to help them to understand about conservation management and to see a wide range of animals and plants in their natural habitat.

Chapter 2 Farming and the Countryside

Management body	Reason for designation	Management
Areas of Outstanding Natural Beauty (AONB).	In 2008 there were 49 AONB in England, Wales and Northern Ireland designated by Natural England for England, and the equivalent bodies in Wales and Northern Ireland. They are areas of countryside which have significant landscape value. AONB have a number of aims: • To conserve and enhance the natural beauty of the landscape. • To provide an area for enjoyment of the countryside. • To look after the interests of the local people.	• They are managed much like National Parks through planning controls and practical countryside management. • They are the responsibility of the local authority they are in. Some local authorities have set up conservation boards who manage the AONB such as the South Downs and Mendip Hills. In other local authorities the AONB management is run by the local authority planning department. • Each of the AONB has a management plan.
Environmentally Sensitive Areas (ESA).	These are agricultural areas which have been designated as they need special protection because of their landscape, wildlife or historical value. The scheme was introduced by Defra in 1987 in areas of the country including the Cotswold hills and the Essex coast, as it was felt that new farming methods were ruining the countryside.	• In these areas farmers were given grants to protect the environment such as to keep hedges, replace or maintain field ponds and to repair stone walls. The farmers had to apply for the grants and Defra ensured that the farmers used the money appropriately. • The scheme has now been replaced by the Environmental Stewardship Scheme which all farmers can be part of.
Wildlife reserves.	Wildlife reserves or nature reserves are cared for by the Wildlife Trust. There are 2200 nature reserves in the UK. Nature reserves are areas where wildlife is protected because of its own value. The reserves are very varied but come into three categories: • The 'natural environment', this is the countryside part of the Wildlife Trust from coppiced woodland to chalk downland. • The 'industrial environment', these are the relics of our industrial past such as quarries, railway cuttings and canals. • There are also planned reserves which are like planted gardens and have been set up to be a showcase of fauna and flora typical of the UK.	• Some of the reserves are owned by the Wildlife Trust; some the trust manages for others. • The prime management objective is conservation of wildlife. • Recreational value of the areas is now being encouraged. • Many of the reserves have a visitor centre where people can find out more about the reserve. Leaflets and information boards are available to ensure that visitors are well educated before they go into the reserve, refreshments are usually available and wildlife-friendly gifts can be purchased. • In the reserves, the visitors are asked to keep to the marked paths so that fragile habitats are not trampled on. There are also bird hides so that visitors can view animals without disturbing them.

Exam Tip

- You may be asked to describe a distribution on a map such as the distribution of National Parks. You should start with general points.
- Your answer should then become more specific.
- If data is asked for, you will lose a mark if you don't include it.
- If data is not requested you should still include some as you will be given credit.

ACTIVITY

On a map of the UK, mark the location of an example of each of the management bodies. Annotate the map with the reason for their designation and the ways that they are managed.

Exam Tip

Make sure that you know all of the designations listed in the table.

Exam Tip

Make sure you know some brief facts about their designation and their management.

Unit 3 The Human Environment

How are the pressures and conflicts being managed in Dartmoor National Park?

Dartmoor National Park covers 853 square kilometres in the south-west of England. It became a National Park in 1951 and has over eight million visitors a year.

Visitors to the National Park can cause pressures on and conflicts between the different groups of people who use the park. The National Park is run by the Dartmoor National Park Authority (DNPA) who employ a large workforce to ensure the smooth running of the park. The Park Rangers are the people who have to ensure visitor enjoyment but also ensure that the local environment is maintained.

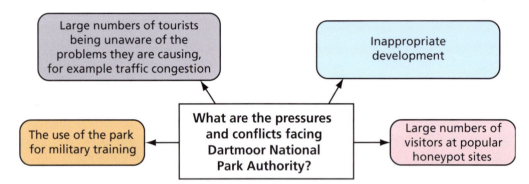

Public information
- There are a number of information centres around the National Park. The High Moorland Visitor Centre, Princeton, is open all year round. The four other centres are open from April until March. The DNPA in 1996 set up its Moor Care Programme to make visitors more aware of the damage they cause.
- Special interest groups are encouraged to talk to the DNPA about their plans so that problems/conflicts can be sorted out before they occur. Such groups include British Canoe Union and South Devon Hang Gliding Club. Various codes of conduct/guidance for recreational activities have been produced by the DNPA and all groups who use the park must adhere to them.

Improving traffic congestion and encouraging visitors not to use their cars
- Through traffic is encouraged to use the A38 and A30 not the A382. The villagers of Moretonhampstead have seen a marked improvement in their quality of life.
- Between 1985 and 1994 traffic increased by 42%.
- Between 1995 and 2002 the increase was 1%.
- The DNPA is also paying towards the provision of some public transport in the area which otherwise would be withdrawn as it is not economically viable. The number 72 from Bovey Tracey to Newton Abbot and the number 82 Exeter to Plymouth transmoor link are two of these services.
- A Sunday rover ticket has also been introduced with 10% more passengers in 2004 than 2002.
- Okehampton train station has been reopened for passengers to encourage visitors to travel by train not by car.
- The Dartmoor Freewheeler bike bus runs from April until the end of September. Buses collect people and their bikes for £5 a trip. The service operates on a rota basis from Saltram to Princetown, Newton Abbot to Mardon Down, Plymouth to Okehampton and Buckfastleigh to Postbridge.
- A speed limit of 40 miles an hour has been introduced on 90 miles of open moorland roads.

Chapter 2 Farming and the Countryside

The management of military training in the park
In Dartmoor, 11% of the land area is owned by the army and used for training purposes. This can cause conflicts with both local people and visitors. Every year a group of interested parties, including representatives from the army, the DNPA and Natural England meet to discuss any issues that have arisen. Conflicts that may occur between the visitors and the army are minimised by making the public fully aware of when areas will be closed for military exercises. The military training areas are focused between Okehampton and Princetown. The areas are open for 245 days at Okehampton. The closed days are notified on the internet, in local newspapers and in Dartmoor National Park publications. Most of the training involves infantry work and therefore causes very little disruption to the local residents.

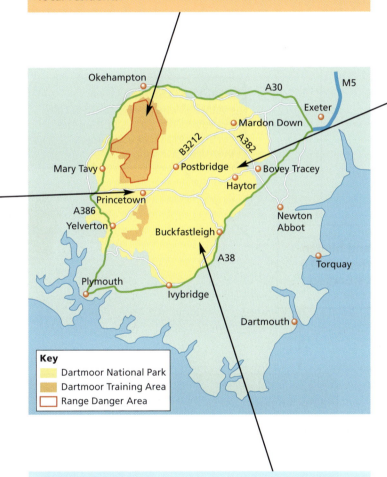

The management of honeypot sites
Most areas of the park can cope with a certain amount of recreational pressure from walkers. However, pressure at honeypot sites is greater and requires appropriate management.

The amount of erosion in popular areas is monitored carefully. There are rangers who are responsible for an area of the park. They monitor their areas by observation and photography and report any erosion problems. If the erosion is serious enough there will be money put aside to deal with the problem.

Haytor Moor is a very popular tourist honeypot but was suffering from a number of problems which have been managed in the following ways:
- The paths to the tor from the car park were very narrow causing erosion. The bracken has been cut back to allow visitors room to roam.
- Erosion gullies are regularly filled in and returfed.
- Patches of bare earth near Haytor quarry have been reseeded.
- Vehicles had been driven on to land beside the car park due to lack of parking spaces; this has damaged the grass. Low grassed banks have been created around the car park's edges. In other areas granite blocks have been used to encircle the car park.

Planning permission
Planning permission can cause many problems and conflicts. The local people will want to be treated like residents in other areas and not have restrictions put on them just because they live in a National Park. Outside of National Parks, planning permission is granted by the local council. In National Parks it is the National Park Authority who have the final say if a development can take place. This can cause resentment and bad feeling between the locals and National Park Authorities. However, in the long run it means that the aims of the National Park are met.

3 Settlement Change

Factors affecting settlements

Physical and human factors affecting the site and situation, growth and shape of settlements

Site: The land on which a settlement is built is called the site
Situation: A settlement's situation is its location relative to its surroundings
Shape: The shape of a settlement is the arrangement of houses within it

Communication – settlements often grew where rivers could be easily crossed. This might be at fords (for example Oxford) or at bridging points. Many large cities were originally sited at the lowest bridging point (the nearest point to the sea that could be bridged); examples include London and Exeter.

Other favourable communication sites were at the junction of valleys or in gaps through hills. Settlements also developed at favourable coastal locations. Ports such as Poole in Dorset grew up around large natural harbours.

Water supply – settlements that are located close to rivers, lakes or springs are called wet-point sites.

Aspect and shelter – in the northern hemisphere, south-facing slopes receive more sun than the north-facing slopes and are therefore warmer.

Dry-point sites – settlements that are sited above the flood plain are called dry-point sites. The city of Ely in Cambridgeshire was originally built on a slightly higher area of land surrounded by marshland.

Physical and human factors affecting the site and situation

Resources – early settlers relied on timber for both fuel and building material. A site close to woodland was therefore an advantage. Stone was also used for building, so proximity to a quarry was also useful. During the Industrial Revolution, coal was in great demand as a power source for factories. Many mining towns sprang up on the coalfields of northern England.

Defence – centuries ago, selecting a site for defence purposes was very important. A castle was often built on high ground overlooking the surrounding countryside. This is the case in Edinburgh. Many settlements are located on the inside of river meanders because they would only need to be protected in one direction. For example, Warkworth.

Figure 1

Exam Tip

- You may be asked to describe a distribution on a map such as the distribution of settlements. You should start with general points.
- Your answer should then become more specific.
- If data is asked for, you will lose a mark if you don't include it.
- If data is not requested you should still include some as you will be given credit.

Chapter 3 Settlement Change

ACTIVITY
Explain the physical and human factors that affect the site and situation of a settlement.

Exam Tip
When answering a question on site and situation, it is a good idea to define the terms in your answer. Extra marks are usually available for this.

Settlement shapes

Nucleated settlements have the individual buildings grouped closely together. They often form at crossroads or route centres.

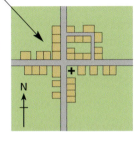

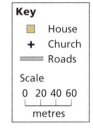

Hint! You will need to be able to recognise the shape of settlements on a map.

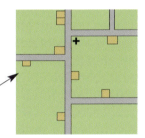

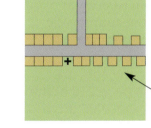

Figure 2 Diagram of settlement shapes

Dispersed settlements have individual buildings spread out. There is usually no obvious centre. They are often farming communities in rural areas.

Linear settlements have buildings on either side of a road. For example, in the valleys of South Wales the villages are restricted in their growth. They line the bottom of the valleys because it is too steep for the houses to be built up the sides of the valleys. Coastal towns are often very linear in shape because they have grown along the coastline.

ACTIVITY
Compare the shape of the settlements shown in Figure 2.

Exam Tip
- When the command word **compare** is used, you should state the similarities between the photographs or figures that have been given. However, examiners at GCSE will also credit comments about the differences (contrasts).
- You may be asked to describe a distribution on a map. You should start with general points.
- Your answer should then become more specific.
- If data is asked for, you will lose a mark if you don't include it.
- If data is not requested you should still include some as you will be given credit.

21

Unit 3 The Human Environment

Changes to rural communities

Counter-urbanisation

Counter-urbanisation is the movement out of cities to rural areas or smaller urban settlements. This process has been happening in MEDCs for the past 50 years.

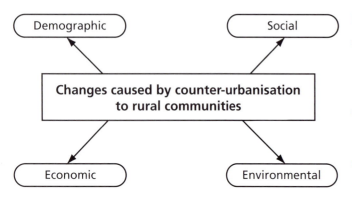

Changes can be beneficial or detrimental.

Demographic changes
- An effect of this movement is the fact that it has created an ageing population in rural areas.
- The people who move out of the countryside are the young and single people who are looking for work and facilities that an urban area can offer. This is shown on the age–sex pyramid for 2005 in Figure 9 on page 218 of the student's book. Between 1985 and 2005 there were major changes in the age structure of rural areas in the UK.
- In some rural areas there was a 30% decrease in the population aged 15–29 and a 25% increase in the numbers aged 40–59.
- The people who tend to move to rural areas are the more affluent who have a young family or the retired.

Social changes
- There can be conflict between the local residents and the newcomers to the area.
- The traditions of the village are not valued by the newcomers therefore there can be a loss in community spirit.
- Many church parishes have been amalgamated as the newcomers might not go to church.
- Local schools have an increase in pupils and are able to stay open.

Economic changes
- House prices in rural areas may rise as demand increases. This may mean that local people cannot afford to buy a house and have to move away from their local area.
- Many of the migrants do not support local businesses and do their shopping in the urban areas where they work.
- Some local services are supported such as the public house and local tradesmen (for example, builders).

Environmental changes
- Many of the migrants still work in urban areas, therefore the journey to work can cause congestion and pollution.
- Villages become ghost towns during the day – there is a loss of community spirit.
- Old, derelict farm buildings are turned into habitable dwellings which add to the aesthetic value and community well-being.

An example of a settlement that has been affected by counter-urbanisation is Austrey in Warwickshire. People moved out of the city of Birmingham and the local town of Tamworth into this village during the 1970s. It caused a growth in population from 300 in 1961 to 1000 in 2001. The environment of the village changed with a number of new housing estates being built, such as St Nicholas Close and Elms Drive, on previous farmsteads. There used to be 18 farms in the village and now only two are left. The buildings of the others have been converted into houses; meaning that the village lost some of its original character. The village school has opened on a new site with 120 children on roll; in 1961 there were 16 children. The village pub, The Bird in Hand, is thriving and has become a meeting place for the local community. Many of the people who live on the new estates work in Birmingham and most families have two cars.

Depopulation of remote rural areas

There has generally been a movement out of rural areas which are classed as remote rural areas for the past 25 years.

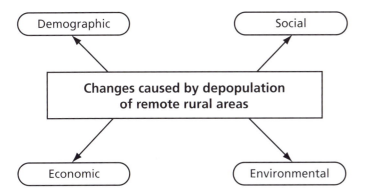

Demographic changes

There has been a decline in population for the age bands up to 40 in all remote rural areas. Young adults leave the area which means that there are fewer young children. The population then develops an older structure.

Economic changes

As the population becomes older there will be less money going into the running of public services such as waste treatment and water. This can cause problems for local councils.

The economy of the area also decreases because as fewer people of working age live there, less money is going into the economy.

Environmental changes

In some remote rural areas there are signs of neglect and derelict buildings, which can be unappealing. The decrease in population is however a bonus for the wildlife of the area.

Social changes

This movement out of remote rural areas has meant that the people who remain there have seen a decline in service provision. In 2001 there were 600,000 people living in what can be classed as remote rural areas; 45% of these people did not live within 4 km of a doctors' surgery, 4 km of a Post Office and were also without a bus service.

This situation will continue to worsen as many Post Offices are closing in rural areas in the UK due to them not being profitable. In Cornwall 25% and in Devon 22% of Post Offices are set to close while the county average for the UK is 18%.

The decline in rural services has also seen the closure of many primary schools such as Satterthwaite and Rusland School and Lowick School, both near Ulverston in the Lake District. They were closed in 2006.

ACTIVITY

Explain the changes that have occurred to rural communities due to rural depopulation and counter-urbanisation. Use examples in your answer.

Exam Tip

Don't be caught out. Learn points for social, economic, demographic and environmental changes.

Exam Tip

For questions that ask for examples, your answer will be marked as follows:

Foundation Tier – Each point will receive a mark. If your answer does not contain a specific point about an example, you will lose one mark.

Higher Tier – If the command word is **outline** or **describe**, these questions will usually be marked out of four marks. Each point will receive a mark. If your answer does not include specific points about an example, you will only receive two marks. If examples are asked for and you only give one you will lose one mark.

Unit 3 The Human Environment

Changing land use in urban areas

Land use in urban areas

Land use in urban areas in the UK has shown a dramatic change over the past 30 years. This is due to two significant trends:

- There has been an increased demand for housing by the UK population.
- There has been deindustrialisation. Manufacturing has moved from urban areas in the UK to LICs where production costs are much lower.

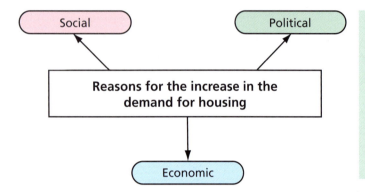

Political
- The population of the UK is increasing. It is predicted to rise by 4.1 million between 2001 and 2021.
- The government has promised that three million new homes will be built by 2020. The growth will take place in certain areas of the country. One of the developments in the south-east is in Bracknell.
- There has been a large influx of EU nationals since the relaxation of borders between EU countries.

Social
- People are now marrying later in life – the average age has gone up from 24 in 1960 to 30 in 2010.
- People are having fewer children and later in life which has also impacted on the type of houses that are wanted. There are now more flats and smaller houses being built.
- There has also been a rise in the number of divorces which means that a family are not living as a group but are living in two different dwellings.
- Many people now live on their own or with their spouse until they are in their 70s and 80s – this means that more houses are needed for the younger generation.

Economic
- The population is wealthier, therefore young people can afford to buy or rent flats at an earlier age and no longer have to live with their parents.
- Until recently people were encouraged to buy their own properties because 100% mortgages were available.

ACTIVITY
Explain the reasons for the increase in demand for housing.

Exam Tip
You could be asked questions that require recall of knowledge. You should learn at least one specific social, economic and political reason.

Chapter 3 Settlement Change

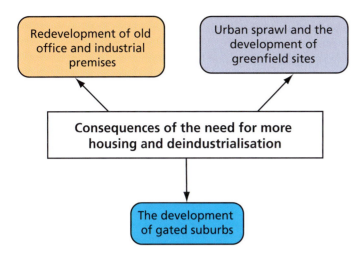

Redevelopment of old factory premises

There has been a major shift in employment in urban areas in the UK with manufacturing industry moving to LICs where production costs are lower. This has led to many buildings being left derelict. The derelict buildings on these sites are either converted into a new use such as housing, known as renewal, or the buildings are knocked down and new ones built, which is known as redevelopment.

A brownfield site that has experienced renewal and redevelopment is in Norwich. It is a large site comprising 17 hectares and is located south-east of Norwich city centre, on the banks of the River Wensum close to the railway station and the football ground at Carrow Road. The site has been redeveloped over a number of years. The redevelopment has seen the building of an entertainment complex including a 14-screen cinema, a large shopping centre and over 200 residential units, many of them apartments built along the river side. New foot and cycle bridges have been built across the river to give better access to the area.

Urban sprawl and the development of greenfield sites

The demand for housing has also been met by building on greenfield sites around the edge of urban areas leading to urban sprawl. Bracknell in Berkshire is seeing significant growth with a large new housing development on a greenfield site to the west of the town. Peacock Farm estate is situated next to the A329M and is close to the M4 for easy access for residents. The development includes 14,000 new homes, 91 acres of country parkland, a doctors' surgery and two primary schools.

ACTIVITY

Figure 3 is a photograph of Salford Quays in Greater Manchester. Draw a sketch of the photograph and annotate examples of redevelopment and renewal.

Figure 3 Salford Quays in Greater Manchester

Unit 3 The Human Environment

The development of gated suburbs
Some areas have seen the development of 'gated suburbs'. This is the concept which originated in countries such as South Africa to protect residents. A number of housing developments, for example in the south-east and the north-west, now have gates to protect them from perceived threats such as burglars. The gated estate below is Walton Drive in Ascot, Berkshire.

Electronic side gate for pedestrians.

Electronic gates which residents can open from homes or with remote controls.

Intercom for visitors to gain entrance.

Redevelopment: This is when buildings in a city, which are no longer of use, are demolished and replaced with buildings that are in current demand
Renewal: This is when old buildings are renovated and brought up to date, combining the best of the old with the new
Brownfield site: This is an area within a city, which is no longer used. It may contain old factories and housing, or it may have been cleared ready for redevelopment
Greenfield site: An area on the edge of the city, which has never been developed in any way

ACTIVITY

Explain the consequences of the increase in demand for housing.

Exam Tip

- You could be asked questions that require recall of knowledge. You should learn specifics points for each of the consequences mentioned.
- You may be asked questions about the consequences of the increase in demand for housing with reference to a photograph or other resource. In this case you will have to apply your knowledge about the consequences to the area shown.

The advantages and disadvantages of brownfield sites

Advantages	Disadvantages
Planning permission is easier to get, the government is actively encouraging the use of these sites.	Complete environmental survey needed because of past usage, this is costly and time consuming.
Infrastructure such as gas, electricity and water is already present.	Perception of contaminated environment puts off prospective buyers.
Easier to market because of access to entertainment and other facilities.	Cities may have social problems – such as anti-social behaviour and crime as well as higher levels of pollution and congestion which could make marketing more difficult.
No building on greenfield so lessens urban sprawl.	Brownfield sites have to be cleared and in some cases decontaminated which adds to the construction costs.
	Land costs are higher as it is closer to the city centre.

The advantages and disadvantages of greenfield sites

Advantages	Disadvantages
Originally unoccupied therefore developers can build as they wish.	Infrastructure such as gas, electricity and water will not be present.
Plenty of space for car parking and landscaping to improve the working environment.	Urban sprawl using up green spaces on the edge of urban areas.
Cheaper land due to being further from the city centre.	It is more difficult to get planning permission as the government tends to be against it.
Lower construction costs as there is nothing to knock down or renew.	Building could disturb natural habitats and wildlife.
Easy to market to potential buyers because of pleasant environment.	Living on the edge of the city may increase the commute for some people.
Access to the development is easier as roads are not congested.	Disruption to local area during construction.
	People may not want to live away from the city centre because of their social life.

ACTIVITIES

1 Explain the difference between redevelopment and renewal.
2 Outline three advantages and three disadvantages of developing on brownfield sites.

Unit 3 The Human Environment

Rapid growth in LICs

Reasons for the rapid growth of urban areas in LICs

Urban areas in LICs have experienced a rapid growth since the 1950s. There are two main reasons for this rapid growth:
- the migration from rural to urban areas
- a high natural increase in population in urban areas.

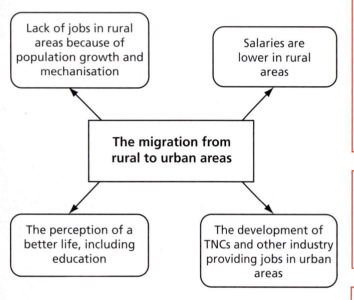

Air pollution
- Air pollution from the two million cars and the 200,000 motorbikes.
- It is predicted that half a million of Cairo's residents will develop serious health problems which will result in premature death.
- In the industrial quarter, Shoubra al-Kheima, where many of the poor people live close to their work, 37% of the residents suffer from lung problems.
- The sun's rays are blocked by smog on the most polluted days which means that many children suffer from a deficiency of vitamin D.
- The lead concentrations in the air from the lead smelters at Shoubra al-Kheima cause a loss of intelligence, at an average of four IQ points.

Noise pollution
- Noise pollution from the two million cars and the 200,000 motorbikes.
- Loudspeakers calling Muslims to prayer.
- Noise of nightclubs on the River Nile. It is particularly bad in the Saraya Al Gezira district.

Land pollution
- The inhabitants of Cairo produce 10,000 tonnes of solid waste a day. Only 60% is collected; the rest is left to rot in streets, canals, drains and neighbourhood dump sites. Rats and other vermin live in plague proportions on the waste dumps. Diseases are carried by the rats and can easily affect the inhabitants of Helwan.
- Large toxic stockpiles of hazardous waste, as much as 50,000 tonnes, from industry which has accumulated in Helwan, Shoubra and Embaba.

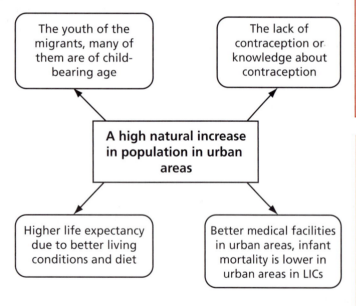

Housing problems
- Approximately 60% of Cairo's population live in shanty-type dwellings. The most famous of these is the 'City of the Dead' or Arafa (cemetery) as it is called by the local residents. This 4-mile long cemetery in eastern Cairo is where people live and work among their dead ancestors. The government has provided some electricity and water standpipes but there is no connection to the sewage system. It is not known how many people live among the gravestones in the 'City of the Dead' but estimates range from 30,000 to one million.
- The government has responded to the housing problem by building cities on the edge of Cairo in the desert. Two of these are 6th of October and 10th of Ramadan. Many Cairo residents, however, want to stay in the city where their jobs are. Another effect of the housing shortage is that young professionals cannot marry because strong social rules say that couples cannot wed until the man can provide a home.

ACTIVITY
Explain the reasons for the rapid growth of urban areas in LICs.

Chapter 3 Settlement Change

The effects of rapid growth on an LIC urban area – Cairo

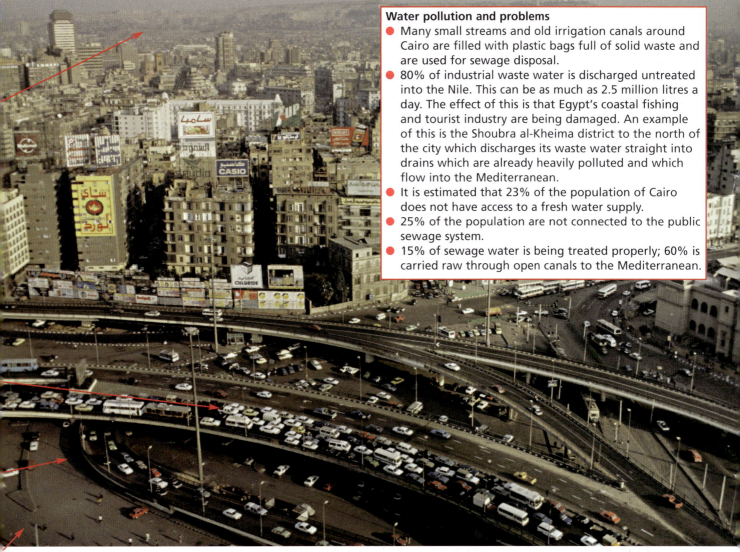

Water pollution and problems
- Many small streams and old irrigation canals around Cairo are filled with plastic bags full of solid waste and are used for sewage disposal.
- 80% of industrial waste water is discharged untreated into the Nile. This can be as much as 2.5 million litres a day. The effect of this is that Egypt's coastal fishing and tourist industry are being damaged. An example of this is the Shoubra al-Kheima district to the north of the city which discharges its waste water straight into drains which are already heavily polluted and which flow into the Mediterranean.
- It is estimated that 23% of the population of Cairo does not have access to a fresh water supply.
- 25% of the population are not connected to the public sewage system.
- 15% of sewage water is being treated properly; 60% is carried raw through open canals to the Mediterranean.

Figure 4 The effects of rapid population growth – Cairo

ACTIVITY
Explain the effects of rapid growth on Cairo.

Case study questions will use the following mark scheme:
Foundation Tier
Level 1 (1–2) A simple answer which has very little description. Could be about anywhere, not linked to any particular study.
Level 2 (3–4) A basic answer with level two being reached by there being descriptive points or a specific point or possibly a weak explanation. The top of the level requires a specific point and some linked descriptive points or a specific point and weak explanation.
Level 3 (5–6) A clear answer with level three being reached by there being a clear explanation or a specific point. The top of the level requires a range of specific points or a number of explanations or a specific point and an explanation.
Higher Tier
Level 1 (1–2) A basic answer which has simple descriptive statements.
Level 2 (3–4) A clear answer with level two being reached by there being an explanation or a specific point. The top of the level requires a range of specific points or a number of explanations or a specific point and an explanation.
Level 3 (5–6) An explicit answer with a range of specific and explained points.

4 Population Change

Population growth and distribution

How is global population changing?

Rapid population growth is a recent phenomenon in the history of the world. It is estimated that in the year zero the world's population was about 300 million. It took 1800 years to grow to one billion. It has only taken 200 years to grow to 6.5 billion and it is still increasing rapidly.

Population in billions	Year reached	Difference in years between each billion
	1804	10,000
	1927	123
	1960	33
	1974	14
	1987	13
	1999	12
	2011	12

Figure 1

Why is population growing rapidly?

The main reason for this rapid growth in population is the reduction in the death rate in LICs and MICs. The birth rate in many of these countries is still high and therefore the population of the continental areas of Africa, South America and Asia continues to grow very rapidly.

Country	Birth rate per thousand	Death rate per thousand	Natural increase per thousand
Mali (Africa)	50	16	34
Laos (Asia)	34	11	23
Paraguay (South America)	29	5	24

By comparison HICs have a low birth and death rate giving a slowly increasing or even a decreasing population.

ACTIVITY

Why do some LICs have low death rates?

30

Chapter 4 Population Change

How is the global population distributed?

Population density is the number of people who live in a defined area. Population distribution is where the people are.

- World population distribution is uneven.
- Places which are sparsely populated contain few people.
- Places which are densely populated contain many people.

Sparsely populated places
- High land that is mountainous and inhospitable, for example Himalayas.
- Areas with few resources tend to be sparsely populated, for example the Sahel.
- Areas with extreme climates of cold or hot tend to be sparsely populated, for example Siberia and the Sahara Desert.
- Countries with unstable governments tend to have lower population densities as people migrate, for example Afghanistan.
- Limited job opportunities cause some areas to be sparsely populated, for example Amazon Rainforest.

Densely populated places
- Low land which is flat, for example Ganges Valley in India.
- Areas rich in resources (coal or oil for instance) tend to densely populated, for example France.
- Areas with temperate (not extreme) climates tend to be densely populated as there is enough rain and heat to grow crops, for example the UK.
- Countries with stable governments tend to have a high population density, for example Singapore.
- Good job opportunities encourage high population densities, particularly in large cities in HICs and LICs around the world.

What are birth and death rates?

ACTIVITY

State two human and two physical reasons for places being sparsely populated.

A birth rate higher than death rate leads to a natural increase in populations

Birth rate more than death rate: population increases

Birth rate and death rate the same: population remains the same

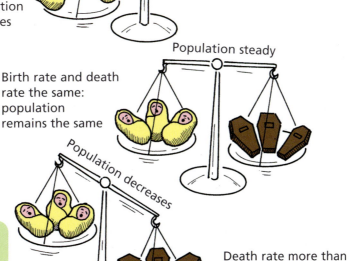

Death rate more than birth rate: population decreases

Remember, population doesn't always have to go up. It can also go down.

Exam Tip

- You may be asked to describe a distribution on a map. You should start with general points.
- Your answer should then become more specific.
- If data is asked for, you will lose a mark if you don't include it.
- If data is not requested you should still include some as you will be given credit.

Figure 2 The balance between birth and death rates

Unit 3 The Human Environment

What causes birth and death rates to change?

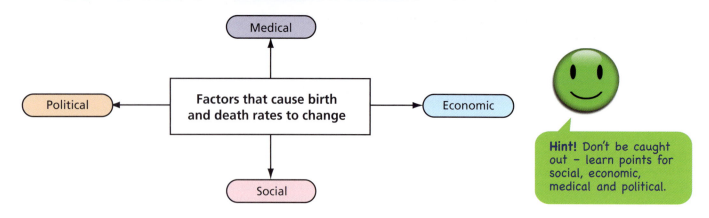

Hint! Don't be caught out – learn points for social, economic, medical and political.

Medical
- In HICs new treatments, such as medicines to treat cancer, are continually being invented to combat diseases, which lead to longer lives.
- Inoculations for childhood diseases have rapidly decreased the death rates in many LICs.
- In March 2006, The Health Foundation launched a 3-year programme dedicated to improving the quality of healthcare for mothers and babies in Malawi. It aims to reduce the mortality rate among children under 5 years of age by two-thirds by 2015.

Social
- Educating women provides them with information on ways to control fertility. It also increases the time they spend in school and in further education; this leads to a greater chance of full-time careers.
- Consequently, it is likely to raise the average age of marriage and delay their child-bearing age.
- People are now marrying later in life, the average age has gone up from 24 in 1960 to 30 in 2010.
- Some religions such as Catholic and Muslim do not allow birth control which will generally lead to a higher birth rate.

Economic
- It is expensive to have children. In the UK it costs an average of £186,032 to raise a child from birth to the age of 21. Increasingly in HICs, couples do not want to change their lifestyle in order to have children.
- Death rate in the UK is strongly affected by poverty. The death rate for Glasgow is more than twice as high as Wimborne, Dorset. The male death rate in Glasgow was the highest in Britain at 1420 per 100,000. Wimborne had the lowest death rate, at 700 per 100,000.

Political
- Countries such as China and India have attempted to decrease birth rates through the introduction of family planning programmes.
- Other countries, such as France and Singapore are giving incentives to increase the birth rate because they are worried that the population of their country is ageing and will not have a large enough workforce.
- As there will not be a large enough working population to support the dependent population, taxes will have to rise and pension entitlements fall.

Exam Tip
- You may be asked to describe a distribution on a map such as the distribution of global population. You should start with general points.
- Your answer should then become more specific.
- If data is asked for, you will lose a mark if you don't include it.
- If data is not requested you should still include some as you will be given credit.

ACTIVITY
Draw a mind map showing reasons for birth rate changes.

Chapter 4 Population Change

What are the characteristics of the demographic transition model?

Figure 3 describes the way the total population of an area changes through time because of differences in birth and death rates.

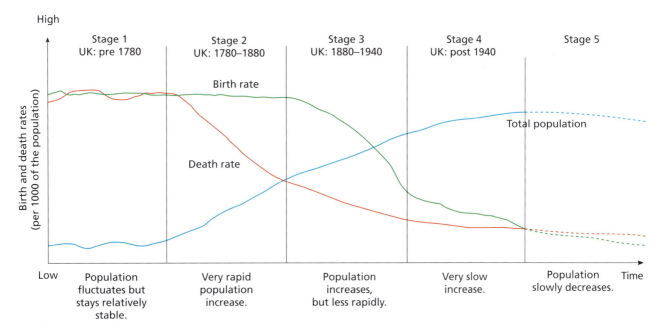

Figure 3 The demographic transition model

	Stage 1	Stage 2	Stage 3	Stage 4	Stage 5
Birth rate	High	High	Falls	Low and fluctuates	Low
Death rate	High and fluctuates	Falls	Low	Low	Low but higher than birth rate
Population change	Small growth	Rapid growth	Slower growth	Stable	Slow decrease
Places	Amazon tribes	Poor LICs, e.g. Mali	Developing LICs, e.g. Taiwan	HICs, e.g. UK	Central and east Europe, e.g. Germany and Estonia
UK	Before 1750	1750–1880	1880–1950	Post-1950	Still in stage 4, possibly stage 5 in the future if birth rate rises
Stage characteristics	Subsistance agriculture, high infant mortality	Improved food supply, no birth control, some medical advancement, little secondary education	Better living conditions, improving health care and hygiene, birth control, rapid urbanisation	High standards of living, education for all, high level of tertiary employment, late marriage	Very low birth rates due to desire for 'economic well-being'

ACTIVITY

Draw a sketch diagram of the demographic transition model and annotate it with characteristics of the birth and death rates.

Hint! You may be asked to explain the birth and death rate in each stage in an exam.

33

Unit 3 The Human Environment

What are the physical and human factors affecting the distribution and density of population in China and the UK?

China

The distribution and density of population has been greatly influenced by physical and human conditions.

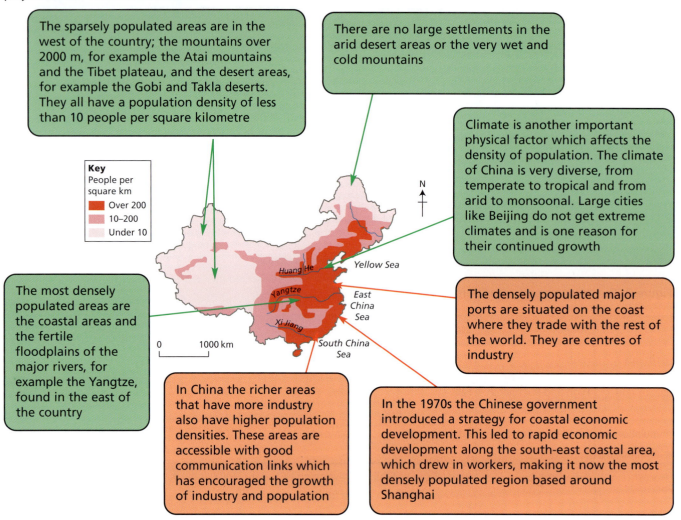

Figure 4 How physical and human conditions have influenced the density and distribution of population in China

ACTIVITY

Outline the human and physical factors that have influenced population distribution in China.

Exam Tip

For questions that ask for examples, your answer will be marked as follows:

Foundation Tier – Each point will receive a mark. If your answer does not contain a specific point about an example, you will lose one mark.

Higher Tier – If the command word is **outline** or **describe**, these questions will usually be marked out of four marks. Each point will receive a mark. If your answer does not include specific points about an example, you will only receive two marks. If examples are asked for and you only give one you will lose one mark.

Chapter 4 Population Change

The UK

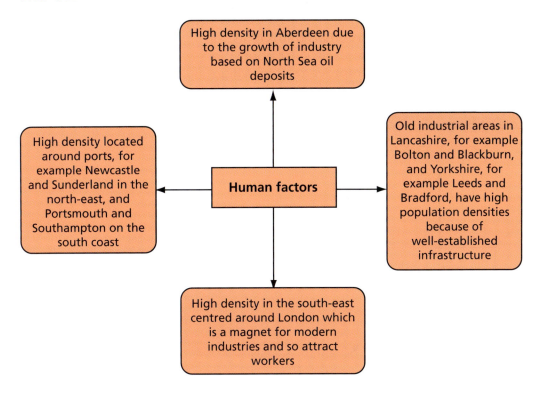

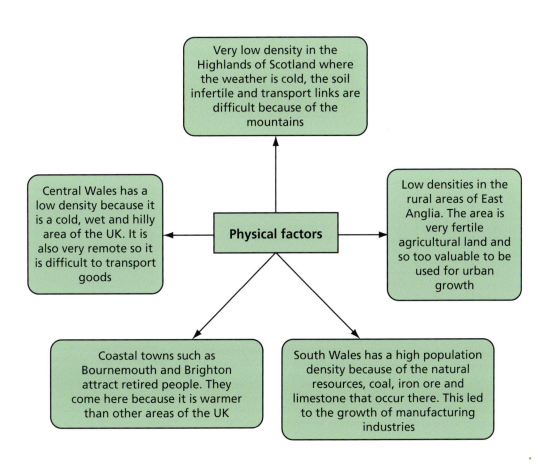

Unit 3 The Human Environment

What has been done to reduce China's birth rate?

In 1979 China had a quarter of the world's population. Two-thirds of its population was under the age of 30. The government saw strict population control as essential to economic reform and to an improvement in living standards, so the one-child family policy was introduced.

Couples were only allowed one child and were given a 'one-child certificate' entitling them to a package of benefits.

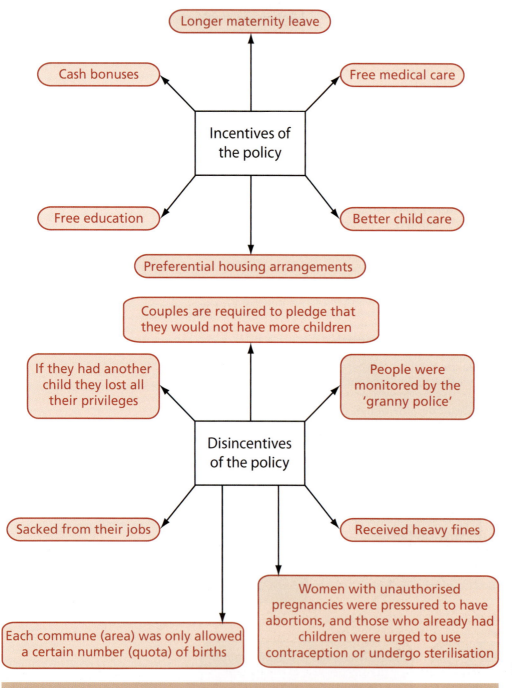

Recent changes to the one-child policy
- In rural areas, a second child is generally allowed after 5 years, but this usually only applies if the first child is a girl. A third child is allowed among some ethnic minorities and in remote, underpopulated areas.
- For urban residents and government employees, the policy is strictly enforced, with a few exceptions. The exceptions include families in which the first child has a disability or both parents work in high-risk occupations (such as mining) or are themselves from one-child families.

Exam Tip

You could be asked questions that require recall of knowledge. You should learn specific points for incentives and disincentives.

Chapter 4 Population Change

What has been done to increase Singapore's birth rate?

In 1987 Singapore's government introduced the 'three or more policy' which gave people incentives to have more children. It has not been very successful as although the birth rate initially increased from nine per thousand to a peak of 13 per thousand in 2003, it had dropped back to nine per thousand in 2008.

ACTIVITY

Draw spidergrams for the incentives and disincentives for the Singaporean policy.

Incentives that are offered to parents	Disincentives for parents with two or fewer children
A cash gift of $3000 each for first and second child.	Couples with no children are not entitled to buy anything more than a three-room flat.
A cash gift of $6000 each for third and fourth child.	No choice of schools so their education might suffer.
3 months maternity leave for mothers.	They do not receive financial packages offered by the government.
3 days of paternity leave on the birth of the first four children for fathers.	
5 days of paid childcare leave a year.	
Parents can live in large flats.	

Characteristics of population

The characteristics of population on a local scale including age, gender, ethnic, religious and occupational structure

A census is a count of all people and households in the country. It provides population statistics from a national to neighbourhood level. The last census for England and Wales was on 29 April 2001. The next will take place on 27 March 2011 and will involve around 25 million households.

The census gives information on a number of population characteristics:

- **Population size:** an accurate count of the population in each local area helps the government to calculate the funding it allocates each local authority and health authority. In turn, these authorities use census information when planning services within their areas.
- **Population structure:** it is helpful if local councils know the percentage of young or elderly in their community then they can fit the services they provide to particular age group.
- **Population gender:** this is the proportion of males to females in the community.
- **Ethnic group:** an ethnic group is a group of people who have similar cultural characteristics of language, colour, religion and nationality. Information on ethnic groups helps local government to allocate resources and plan programmes to take account of the needs of minority groups.
- **Occupational structure:** the census shows how many people work in different occupations (jobs) and industries throughout the country, helping government and businesses to plan jobs and training policies.
- **Religious structure:** the main groups in the UK are Christian, Muslim, Hindu, Buddhist and atheist.

The census also gives information on other characteristics such as health, housing and transport.

Exam Tip

You may be asked to describe, understand or to interpret census data.

37

Unit 3 The Human Environment

Comparison of population pyramids for three countries at different levels of development

Characteristics	LIC (Philippines)	MIC (Brazil)	HIC (Germany)
Shape	Triangle-shaped pyramid. A wide base, narrowing rapidly.	Still pyramid shaped but more even sided with steps not decreasing as rapidly as LIC.	Pyramid shape is lost with a bulging middle and a decreased base.
Birth rate	Very high as pyramid base is very wide.	Still very high but starting to decrease.	Birth rate has been declining for many years with each step below 25 years showing a decrease.
Death rate	Very high but starting to decrease.	High, but not as high as Philippines.	Low, but stable.
Growth rate	Very high, 2.1% annually.	High, 1.4%.	Negative growth, –0.1%.
Stage of demographic transition model	2	3	4 or 5
Age structure	Youthful population.	Still numerous young people but an increasing amount of middle aged.	Ageing population.
The future	Population will continue to grow as the high proportion of young people reach reproductive age.	The proportion of elderly will increase and the birth rate will decrease as living conditions improve.	The proportion of elderly will continue to increase. Immigration might be encouraged to increase the workforce.

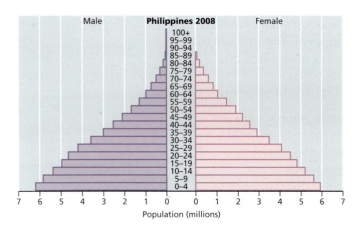

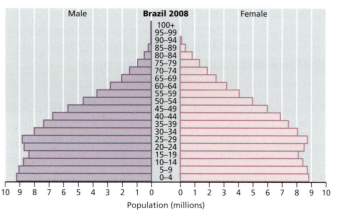

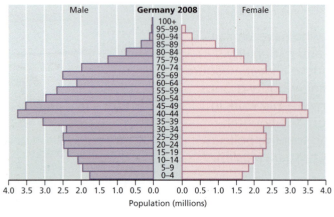

ACTIVITY

Draw sketch pyramids for a LIC, MIC and HIC. Annotate the sketches with comments about the age structure.

Chapter 4 Population Change

What are the consequences of youthful and ageing populations?

People live longer, more houses needed using up large amounts of land.

Money spent on education will be cut to finance the elderly.

Fewer people will be unemployed as the percentage of elderly increases.

Taxes are likely to increase to pay for services and pensions.

Pension age will have to increase. At present the old-age pension is paid at age 65. This will increase in steps to 68 in 2046.

Much greater demand for health care and residential care homes, which are expensive and may lead to people having to sell their home to pay for care.

There will be a growth in the leisure industry with firms wanting to grab the 'grey pound'.

The elderly work without pay in places such as charity shops.

Figure 5 An ageing population

ACTIVITY
Explain what is meant by the grey pound.

Large percentage of under 15s in LICs puts a strain on the economy, particularly with food, education and health.

Childhood diseases such as measles and diarrhoea can be fatal as hospitals and doctors are non-existent in the poor LICs.

There is a large active workforce which will be available to aid economic growth in the future.

A large workforce who cannot get jobs leads to begging in the streets.

Many children to look after their parents so money does not need to be spent on care for the elderly.

Figure 6 A youthful population

39

Unit 3 The Human Environment

What are the advantages and disadvantages of an ageing population in Japan?

Disadvantages

Workforce

- The labour force in the 15–24 age bracket, which stood at more than eight million in 1990, will have shrunk to 5.3 million by 2015.
- At Tokyo's Narita Airport, the marshals who direct passengers to the passport control queue are mostly of pensionable age.
- Taxi drivers and small-shop keepers are more likely than not to be grey-haired pensioners, as is the staff on the Tokyo subway.
- In 2025 there will be only two workers paying taxes to support the pensioners compared to nearly six workers in 1990.
- The shortage of Japanese workers means that there are now two million foreign workers living in Japan; 200,000 of them illegally.
- Men are being encouraged to work after retirement, and women are being encouraged to work.

Pensions

- Pension reforms made in 2005.
- The age of retirement rising from 60 to 65 by 2030.
- Higher pension contributions from the employers, employees and the government.
- Pensions are still likely to fall unless birth rates increase rapidly.

Health care

- The number of people living in nursing homes or care homes is increasing. Paying for caring for the elderly accounts for half of Japan's health budget.
- In 2000 a tax on over-40s was introduced to help pay for equipment such as wheelchairs and sending carers to private homes and retirement institutions to help the elderly.
- A new health insurance scheme for the over-75s was introduced in 2008. It has been nicknamed the 'hurry up and die' scheme. Under recent changes the fee the hospital receives from the government for a patient goes down after 100 days as an incentive to shorten hospital stays.
- There has been an increase in the number of nursing homes but nowhere near enough have been built to house the number of people who need them.

ACTIVITY

Explain two advantages and two disadvantages of an ageing population on Japan.

Advantages

The greying yen

- There is a 'grey boom' in Japan.
- Japan's pensioners are spending more on luxury goods, travelling, and indulging their taste for expensive foods.
- With so many old people spending their incomes this could lead to a growth in the economy.

Technology

- The greying of Japan has led to a technological explosion.
- It has inspired an array of gadgets for people who are worried about elderly relatives. They include: an online kettle that automatically sends emails to up to three people when it is switched on and internet-linked sensors that can be attached to everyday items such as fridge doors and bathroom mats.

Exam Tip

Case study questions will use the following mark scheme:

Foundation Tier

Level 1 (1–2) A simple answer which has very little description. Could be about anywhere, not linked to any particular study.

Level 2 (3–4) A basic answer with level two being reached by there being descriptive points or a specific point or possibly a weak explanation. The top of the level requires a specific point and some linked descriptive points. Or a specific point and weak explanation.

Level 3 (5–6) A clear answer with level three being reached by there being a clear explanation or a specific point. The top of the level requires a range of specific points or a number of explanations or a specific point and an explanation.

Higher Tier

Level 1 (1–2) A basic answer which has simple descriptive statements.

Level 2 (3–4) A clear answer with level two being reached by there being an explanation or a specific point. The top of the level requires a range of specific points or a number of explanations or a specific point and an explanation.

Level 3 (5–6) An explicit answer with a range of specific and explained points.

5 A Moving World

Population movement

What are the different types of population movement?

People migrate to get away from something they do not like (a **push** factor), or may be attracted to another area that is of greater benefit to them (a **pull** factor).

Migration: the movement of people from one area to another, with the intention of remaining there permanently or semi-permanently

Push factors include:
- Natural disasters such as volcanic eruptions or floods
- Harsh climates
- War and political conflicts
- Lack of jobs leading to poverty
- Poor or short supply of housing
- Lack of medical facilities

Pull factors include:
- Hazard-free areas of the world
- Political asylum, freedom of speech
- Higher living standards and plenty of available housing
- Employment opportunities
- Good medical and welfare services

Figure 1 Push and pull factors

Short-term population movements can vary in time, usually less than a year. They involve a circulatory movement which may involve a change of residence. This would include people going on holiday, gap-year students and commuters.

ACTIVITIES

1. Explain three pull factors which attract migrants to an area.
2. Explain three push factors which lead to migrants leaving an area.

Exam Tip

You might be asked to define the following terms:
- **Long-term migration:** a permanent movement.
- **Short-term migration:** more than a year but not permanent.
- **Immigration:** the movement of people into a country.
- **Emigration:** the movement of people out of a country.

Exam Tip

When the command word **compare** is used, you should state the similarities between the photographs or figures that have been given. However, examiners at GCSE will also credit comments about the differences (contrasts).

41

Unit 3 The Human Environment

How can migration be classified?

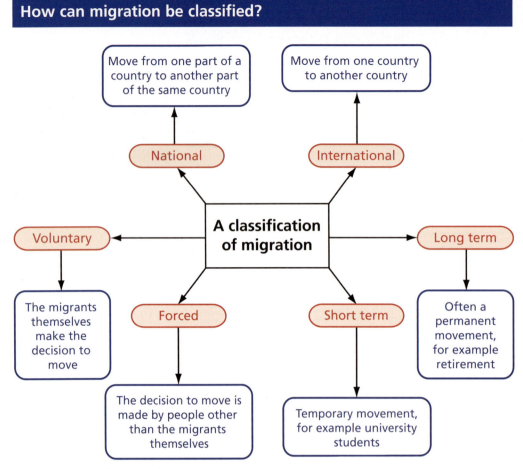

Figure 2 A classification of migration

ACTIVITY

Give a named example of each of the migrations shown in Figure 2.

Exam Tip

- You will need to be able to describe the pattern of migration flows shown on a map.
- You may be asked to describe a distribution on a map. You should start with general points.
- Your answer should then become more specific.
- If data is asked for, you will lose a mark if you don't include it.
- If data is not requested you should still include some as you will be given credit.

Flows of population

What have been the main migration flows into and within Europe since 1945?

Flows into Europe

- After Second World War, many European countries needed labour to repair damage and to help their economies recover.
  - France encouraged workers from its colonies in north Africa such as Algeria and Senegal.
  - Germany attracted many workers from Turkey.
  - The UK's immigrants mostly came from the Commonwealth countries of India, Pakistan and the Caribbean.
  - The Netherlands gained workers, most notably from Indonesia.
- Between 1960 and 1990, European countries received political migrants who were looking for safety:
  - Spain gained many dentists from Argentina and Uruguay.
  - Brazilians went to Portugal seeking jobs in marketing and health care.

Flows within Europe

- After the fall of the 'iron curtain' in 1989 there was a large movement of people from east Europe to west Europe.
- The relaxation in boundaries and the increase in the member countries of the EU has lead to migration between these countries. In particular, citizens of new member states in eastern Europe moving to Germany, France and the UK. In 2008 there were 700,000 Polish people working in the UK.
- Movement of people from northern Europe, Scandinavians and British in particular, seeking the sun of the Mediterranean.

ACTIVITY

On a map of the world, plot the main migration flows into and within Europe.

42

Chapter 5 A Moving World

The social and economic impacts of international population movements on the country of origin and the host country

POSITIVE IMPACTS

- The development of Polish shops on many British high streets adds to the cultural mix of the British society.

- The migrant workers add a considerable amount to consumer spending in the UK. The average migrant worker earns £20,000 per year of which £6000–7000 is disposable income.

- Migrant workers will do low-paid jobs that British workers won't, such as fruit and crop picking.

- Migrants are generally in their 20s and 30s making the UK's workforce younger, therefore easing the pension burden.

The social and economic impacts of international population movements on the host country (UK)

NEGATIVE IMPACTS

- In Cambridgeshire the police force has to deal with 100 different languages. This has cost £800,000 for translators.

- There has been an impact on the welfare state as 27,000 child benefit applications have been approved. Some of these children do not live in the UK but migrant workers are allowed to claim benefit for them.

POSITIVE IMPACTS

- Increase in salaries has meant that people have a higher standard of living and can afford luxury goods.

- To encourage them to stay in Poland, 100 scientists and researchers have each received a one-off payment of £5000. This is equal to 10 months' pay.

- In 2007 monthly salaries in Poland increased by 9% due to a shortage of workers.

The social and economic impacts of international population movements on the country of origin (Poland)

NEGATIVE IMPACTS

- Many Polish villages are suffering from rural depopulation due to the number of migrants.

- The birth rate in Poland has decreased. This is due to the average age of migrants being in the reproductive age group.

- In some areas of Wroclaw a quarter of all anaesthetists have emigrated.

- In 2007, 35% of jobs in the construction industry could not be filled due to a shortage of workers caused by migration.

ACTIVITY
Without using your books, outline two social and two economic impacts on Poland.

Exam Tip
You could be asked questions that require recall of knowledge. You should learn specific positive and negative points for social and economic impacts.

Unit 3 The Human Environment

Factors enabling population movement

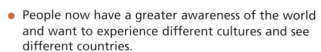

How has the development of e-technology enabled people to move?

- People now have a greater awareness of the world and want to experience different cultures and see different countries.
- People are able to look for work and to find accommodation in other countries very easily using the internet.
- People can keep in close contact with family and friends when they are living abroad.
- People can book flights and other forms of transportation easily on the internet. Thus making it easier to move around the world.
- People can still buy their favourite products on the internet, even if they are not available in the country they have moved to.

How have developments in transport enabled people to move?

- The availability of faster modes of transport has allowed people to move more easily.
- Places now do not seem as far away as they used to as the time to reach them has got less.
- Budget airlines like Ryanair and easyJet allow people to move around the world much more cheaply and therefore more movements are occurring.
- There has also been a major improvement in road and rail services. The opening of the Channel Tunnel has made it very easy to take a car or use the train to cross the English Channel. High-speed rail and motorways link the major cities in Europe. The French TGV train takes only 2 hours to travel between Paris and Lyon.

ACTIVITY

How has transport development affected short-term population flows?

Exam Tip

For questions that ask for examples, your answer will be marked as follows:

Foundation Tier – Each point will receive a mark. If your answer does not contain a specific point about an example, you will lose one mark.

Higher Tier – If the command word is **outline** or **describe**, these questions will usually be marked out of four marks. Each point will receive a mark. If your answer does not include specific points about an example, you will only receive two marks. If examples are asked for and you only give one you will lose one mark.

Chapter 5 A Moving World

Year	Type of Transport	Speed (kilometres per hour)
1750	Stagecoach	11
1800	Stagecoach	24
1800	Rail	25
1850	Rail	100
1900	Rail	135
1950	Rail	160
1950	Plane	500
2000	Rail	208
2000	Plane	850

ACTIVITIES

1 Work out how far you would have been able to travel in 5 hours in 1800, 1900 and 2000.
2 If you were travelling from London where would you have been able to reach in 1 hour in 1800, 1900 and 2000?

How has the relaxation of national boundaries enabled population movement?

- Workers are free to move between the 27 member countries of the EU. They just need a passport or identity card.
- Movement within the EU has become easier but it is getting harder for migrants to enter it legally from other parts of the world.
- The UK introduced an entry points system in 2008. Highly skilled economic migrants are still welcome in the UK as long as they reach the pass mark of 75 points.

Unit 3 The Human Environment

Reasons for short-term population flows

Types of short-term population flows

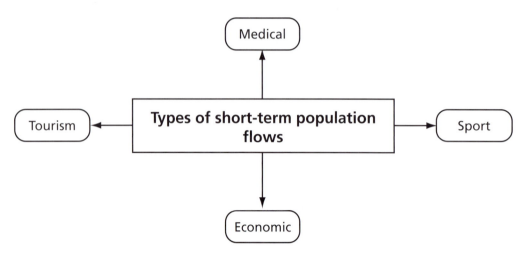

A combination of push and pull factors influence short-term population movements.

Medical

Examples include having dental work done in countries like Hungary and the Czech Republic, and plastic surgery in South Africa.

Push factors	Pull factors
• Unhappy with the National Health Service because waiting lists are lengthening and demand is not being met.	• The treatment is much cheaper abroad.
• Poorly maintained hospitals in the UK.	• Modern medical facilities with state-of-the-art equipment which are clean and well stocked.
• British hospitals are perceived to be dirty and patients feel that they are not well cared for.	• Can be done as part of a package holiday.
• Hospitals are closing down, therefore patients will have longer distances to travel.	• Better patient care with more time spent by doctors and nurses with the patients.
• Patients feel that they are being treated as if they are on a production line.	
• Private health care is expensive in the UK.	

46

Sport

Examples include golfers following the European tour to countries in Europe, Africa and Asia and footballers moving to the Premiership from clubs in other European countries.

Push factors	Pull factors
Low pay.	Financial rewards.
Poor competition in second-rate leagues.	Compete against the best players in the world.
Unsatisfactory quality of life with little entertainment.	Living in places like London, which is a major world city, where entertainment and quality of life are good.

Tourism

This is where people move for short periods of time to destinations outside the places that they normally live and work. The following table shows the push and pull factors that attract UK tourists to France.

Push factors	Pull factors
Climate: Cold and wet English climate.	**Climate:** Hot and dry summer weather and snowy mountainous areas.
Economic: The average worker in the UK has increasingly more disposable income and can afford to have holidays.	**Physical attractions:** Stunning scenery of mountains and beaches such as the Alps and The Vendée.
Media: There are now several TV programmes which are targeted towards tourists. Shows like *Homes in the Sun* and *Sky Travel* make people aware of where they can go and how easy it is to get there.	**Human attractions:** Disneyland Resort Paris and cultural attractions such as the Pont du Gard, the chateaux of the Loire and the Roman amphitheatre in Nîmes.
	Transport: France is a very accessible country because they have first-class transport links with countries in Europe and worldwide. Many new airports, such as at Bergerac, linked to Ryanair and easyJet, have developed in France in the past decade.

Unit 3 The Human Environment

Economic

A short-term population flow. An economic migrant moving from Poland to the UK

Motives for migrating

- The main motive for economic migrants is an increase in wealth. Workers from eastern European countries such as Poland, Latvia and Romania have moved to the UK in search of better-paid jobs.
- Some of the migrants only come for very short periods of time to coincide with seasonal jobs such as fruit or vegetable picking. They stay for a few months in the spring and summer and then go back to their families with enough money to see them through the winter. These migrants are very common in rural areas of the UK such as Norfolk and Lincolnshire.
- Other migrants, normally educated, come for a longer period of time and look for full-time positions in jobs like health care and education.

What are the problems that the migrant encounters and what solutions are there?

Problems for economic migrants	Solution to the problems
The less-educated migrants often do not speak English very well and can be taken advantage of by unscrupulous employers who don't pay them a fair wage.	This would not happen if the migrant could speak English. There are classes available all over the country where they can learn basic English.
Poland is a much more rural country than England. The migrants often find it difficult to adjust to the noise and speed of English city life. This can lead to stress and many return to Poland because of homesickness.	Polish immigrants now comprise one of the largest ethnic groups in London. The Greater London boroughs of Acton, Balham, Brixton, Ealing, Earls Court, and Hammersmith have become known as 'Polish towns'. This 'living together' helps new migrants to overcome their home sickness for rural areas.
Houses are generally much larger in Poland as there is not such a strain on space. When the Poles come to England they tend to live in flats or small terrace houses which they find very cramped.	As they integrate into English society they spend less time in their flats so don't notice the conditions so much. They put up with the cramped conditions so that they can save money to take back to Poland.
The exchange rate can fluctuate meaning that if the pound may lose value against the zloty, as it did in 2008, the money they earn in England is not worth as much as it used to be in Poland.	The exchange rate has been favourable in the past and might return to a favourable position in the future.

Chapter 5 A Moving World

Retirement migration

What are the reasons for a UK citizen retiring within the UK?
Case study: retirement migration to north Norfolk

- **Cheaper property** – The average house price in 2008 in north Norfolk, part of the East Anglia region, was approximately £200,000, whereas in greater London which supplies a high proportion of the migrants it was over £335,000.
- **The scenery and natural beauty** – Much of the area lies within the north Norfolk Area of Outstanding Natural Beauty (AONB) and the coastline is a designated Heritage Coast.
- **The dry, warm climate** – Norfolk is one of the driest counties in England with the highest summer temperatures in the country and an average annual rainfall of only 625 mm.
- **The relaxed lifestyle** – Attracted by the slower pace of life that is found in rural areas. They are also attracted by lower crime rates, particularly violent crime. Between April 2005 and March 2006, 330 fewer offences of violence were reported.

What are the consequences of a UK citizen retiring within the UK?

Housing
- The increase in the number of in-migrants has lead to the creation of more demand for local housing than the market can supply.
- This increases competition, and houses become more expensive.
- Local people, especially young people are unable to afford these inflated house prices.

Shops and facilities
- Some of the villages in the area have benefited from the retired in-migrants because they support local services and want to be accepted in the local community.
- This means that they shop daily in the local village stores and drink in the local pub. Other villages have changed in character due to the wealth of the retired in-migrants. For example, expensive, designer-label clothes shops (Gunn Hill Clothing Company, Burnham Market) and Michelin star restaurants (Morston Hall, Blakeney).
- As a result the local shops have closed causing many locals to go outside the area for basic necessities.

Population structure
- North Norfolk has an ageing population. This population structure will have massive consequences on north Norfolk.
- Due to the low number of young children, several schools in the area are threatened with closure.
- The ageing population will put a great strain on the medical facilities. A new hospital has been planned for north Norfolk combining a GP surgery, 24 beds and community health services under one roof. There has been a growth in age-related services such as chiropodists and alternative medicines.

Changing village character
- Facilities in the villages are changing to accommodate the older generation.
- New community halls have been built or original ones modernised with National Lottery funding.
- In the past, the halls would have been used for youth clubs and discos.
- Nowadays they are used in the evenings by clubs and societies which are geared towards the older generation such as whist drives and yoga.

Unit 3 The Human Environment

What are the reasons for a UK citizen retiring to Spain?
Case study: retirement migration to Spain

- **Mediterranean climate** – The temperature in Spain is usually a constant 10°C warmer than in the UK.
- **Good communication networks** – The time it takes to fly to Spain is less than the time it takes to drive from London to Manchester. It is also much cheaper to fly there, approximately £50, due to 'no-frills' airlines like easyJet.
- **Lifestyle of Spanish people** – Attracted by the lower crime rates and an absence of 'youth culture'.
- **Lower cost of living** – Important to pensioners on a fixed budget.
- **Cheaper property**.
- **Media enhancement of Spain** – TV programmes such as *A Place in the Sun* make people believe that the 'grass is greener'.
- **Excellent leisure facilities** – For some it may be the availability of sporting activities such as golf courses or bowling greens, for others it may be tea dances, coffee mornings and organised excursions.
- **Free health care** – If you receive a state pension in the UK you will be eligible for free state health care in Spain.
- **Well-networked expatriate community** – People speaking the same language make migrants feel safer.

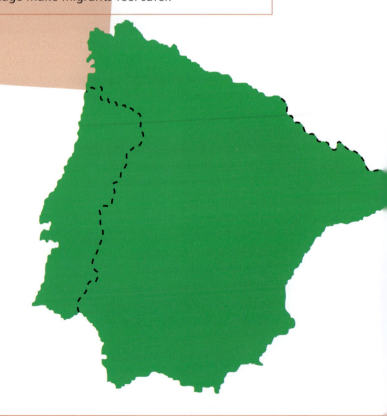

Chapter 5 A Moving World

What are the consequences of a UK citizen retiring to Spain?

Population structure
- Spain has an ageing population. This has been added to by the number of British and other nationalities, particularly Irish, who have migrated there when they retire.
- There will be pressure on the economically active due to the increasing dependent population.

Housing
- There has been a lot of development along the coast of Spain which has caused damage to the coastline.
- This caused the government in 1998 to pass the Coastal Law to try to control beachfront development. Technically, any property built within 106 m of the shore could be demolished.

Water
- The areas of Spain where the expats live such as the Valencia region are known for its shortage of water. Expats buy properties with swimming pools and expect to be able to fill them; this is causing a major problem with water supply in the area.
- Many new housing developments have been built both for holiday homes and for people to buy in their retirement. This was without thought for the lack of water in the area.
- In Murcia, south-east Spain, developers have been given permission to build golf courses, 54 of them in the past 10 years and most of these in the last 3 years. The demand for water is now two and a half times the supply.

Health care
- Many of the British who retire to Spain live on the Costa Blanca. This has caused the cost of health care there to increase dramatically.
- It is estimated that the British expats are costing the local government £800 million a year in health care costs. People who retire early to Spain will now have to pay for their own health care although people over the age of 65 will still be eligible.

Culture
- British newspapers are readily available on the day on which they are published. There are also a number of specific newspapers for the expat community, the largest selling is *El Sun*.
- There are special sections in the supermarkets in these areas for British brands.

ACTIVITY
Explain the reasons for either retirement migration from the UK to Spain or retirement migration from one area of the UK to another area of the UK.

Exam Tip

Case study questions will use the following mark scheme:

Foundation Tier
Level 1 (1–2) A simple answer which has very little description. Could be about anywhere, not linked to any particular study.
Level 2 (3–4) A basic answer with level two being reached by there being descriptive points or a specific point or possibly a weak explanation. The top of the level requires a specific point and some linked descriptive points or a specific point and weak explanation.
Level 3 (5–6) A clear answer with level three being reached by there being a clear explanation or a specific point. The top of the level requires a range of specific points or a number of explanations or a specific point and an explanation.

Higher Tier
Level 1 (1–2) A basic answer which has simple descriptive statements.
Level 2 (3–4) A clear answer with level two being reached by there being an explanation or a specific point. The top of the level requires a range of specific points or a number of explanations or a specific point and an explanation.
Level 3 (5–6) An explicit answer with a range of specific and explained points.

6 A Tourist's World

Growth of the tourist industry

What are the factors that have caused a growth in global tourism?

The growth of global tourism has been caused by a number of factors. The factors can be social, economic and political.

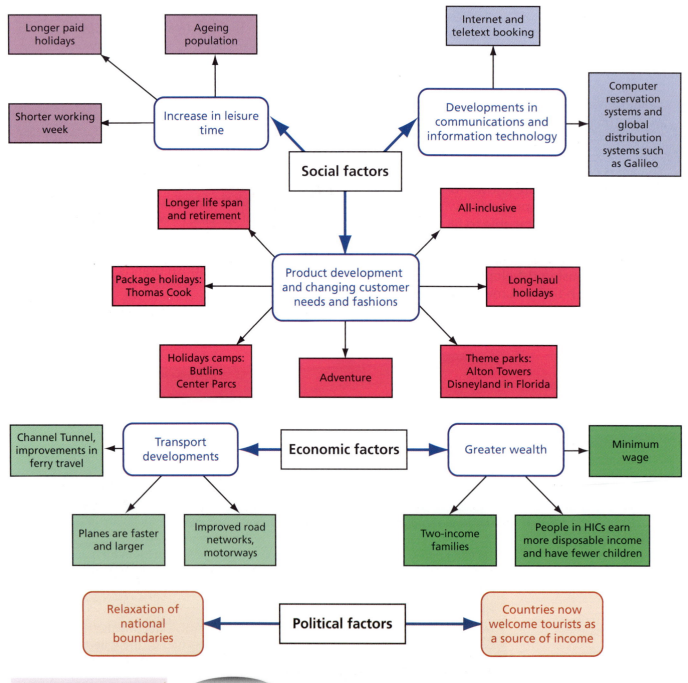

ACTIVITY

Explain the reasons for the growth in global tourism.

You will need to know which are social, economic and political factors although there is some overlap between them.

Chapter 6 A Tourist's World

Holiday destinations offer a variety of physical and human attractions

- **Physical attractions** are the factors about the natural landscape that appeal to people including guaranteed sunshine, white sandy beaches and warm sea if they were looking for a beach holiday. Or mountainous scenery, snow and sunshine if they were looking for a winter sports holiday.

- **Human attractions** are the factors about the built environment that appeal to people including theme parks, ancient monuments and museums.

ACTIVITIES

Look at the two photographs below.

Photograph A

Photograph B

1. Draw out and complete the table below.

Photograph	Physical attractions	Human attractions
A		
B		

2. Compare the physical and human attractions of photograph A and photograph B.
3. Study photographs A and B. What types of holiday could take place in these areas? Give a reason for your answer.

Type of holiday	Description
Package holidays	A package holiday is one that has everything arranged by the tour company such as Thomas Cook. The holiday includes in the price all transportation and accommodation, and usually offers some of the food such as breakfast and evening meal.
Adventure holidays	An adventure holiday is usually for the purpose of challenge, exploration, skills development or thrills. It appeals to young active people or active over-50s who have retired early.
Wedding holidays	It is now possible to get married in exotic locations around the world. Many tour operators will arrange a package tour which includes the honeymoon and the marriage ceremony, often on a palm-fringed, white sandy beach.
Backpacking holidays	Backpacking is a form of low-cost, independent international travel. Backpackers camp, stay in youth hostels or in low-budget hotels. It is generally undertaken by younger travellers, particularly students on a gap year.

Exam Tip

When the command word **compare** is used, you should state the similarities between the photographs or figures that have been given. However, examiners at GCSE will also credit comments about the differences (contrasts).

Exam Tip

Learn a description and an example of each type of holiday.

53

Unit 3 The Human Environment

Resort development

The Butler model of resort development

In 1980, R.W. Butler developed a model for resort development. The model has seven stages which he believes resorts go through as they become tourist destinations.

ACTIVITY
Explain the development of Blackpool in terms of the Butler model of resort development.

Development
- Visitor numbers continue to increase.
- There are still mainly physical and cultural attractions.
- Some built attractions are beginning to develop.
- The host community are becoming more involved with tourism.
- Package holidays will be offered.

Consolidation
- The number of tourists continues to increase but not as quickly.
- Transport routes and access to the resort have been improved.
- The majority of the local people now work in the tourist industry and the local economy relies on tourism income.
- There are many facilities for tourists which are beginning to impact on the environment.

Stagnation
- The facilities and services become old and run down.
- The negative impacts on the environment are becoming more obvious.
- Visitor numbers are declining.
- The host community begins to resent the tourists who have taken over their town.

Exploration
- A small number of tourists visit a destination.
- There are no impacts on the area.
- There are physical and cultural attractions

Involvement
- Visitor numbers start to increase.
- Hotels are built.
- Transport is improved, railway lines built to the resort.

Rejuvenation
- Once in decline many resorts fail to recover.
- Other destinations are successfully regenerated. This usually involves investing a lot of money to improve facilities and amenities.
- The resorts have to be made up-to-date.

Decline
Tourist numbers start to decline dramatically. The local economy is severely affected and many people lose their jobs. The image of the resort suffers and as a result fewer people visit.

Visitor numbers / Time

The table below shows how the Butler model can be applied to Blackpool, a resort on the north-west coast of England.

Stage of model	Date from	Event or fact
Exploration	1735	Blackpool's first guesthouse opened, owned by Edward Whiteside. The only visitors were the landed gentry (rich people) who would ride on the beach and bathe in the sea.
Involvement	1819	Henry Banks opened the Lane's End Hotel which was Blackpool's first hotel. In 1846, the railway line was completed to Blackpool.
Development	1870	Central Pier opened with open-air dancing for everyone. A new promenade was opened to the south which linked the different areas of Blackpool together.
Consolidation	1912	Many attractions were built such as the Grand Theatre, Church Street. Blackpool illuminations were first switched on in 1912.
Stagnation	1986	The Sandcastle (an indoor swimming pool) and Blackpool Zoo opened. But visitor numbers were starting to decline.
Decline	1987	Annual day visits declined from 7.4 million to 3.9 million.
Rejuvenation	2004	11,000,000 people visited Blackpool.

The effects of tourist industry growth

The growth of tourism is having an effect on popular tourist destinations in countries at different levels of development.

These effects can be either positive or negative.

The effects can be economic due to the increase in jobs in primary, secondary and tertiary sectors, or social due to the impact on entertainment facilities or environmental, for example, to footpath erosion.

The effects of tourism on Ayia Napa

Ayia Napa, Cyprus	Social	Economic	Environmental
Positive	- The local youth in Ayia Napa have a much better nightlife due to the clubs that have opened for tourists, for example Monkey Business and the Mambo Bar. - There are more bus services to Larnica, the capital, than there would be if Ayia Napa was still a small fishing village.	- Tourism provides 20% of the GDP of Cyprus. - Jobs are created for the locals at hotels in Ayia Napa, such as the Adams Beach Hotel.	- Lara beach on the Akamas Peninsula has been protected for green turtles to lay their eggs. - All new hotels in Ayia Napa are built with sewage facilities and fresh water supplies.
Negative	- Local fishermen at Ayia Napa have no fish to catch as they have been scared away by the tourists. - The original inhabitants of Ayia Napa have moved away and built themselves a new village on the hill above the town. They were driven away by the behaviour of the tourists.	- The attraction of better paying jobs in the new hotels in Ayia Napa such as the Adams Beach means that there are fewer young people working in agriculture. - Hotels let only about 30% of their rooms in the winter. This means that jobs in hotels are only seasonal.	- There has been a massive building programme with many new hotels being built right next to Nissi beach. - The beach was used by turtles to lay their eggs but they no longer come to this part of Cyprus.

Unit 3 The Human Environment

The effects of tourism on Zanzibar

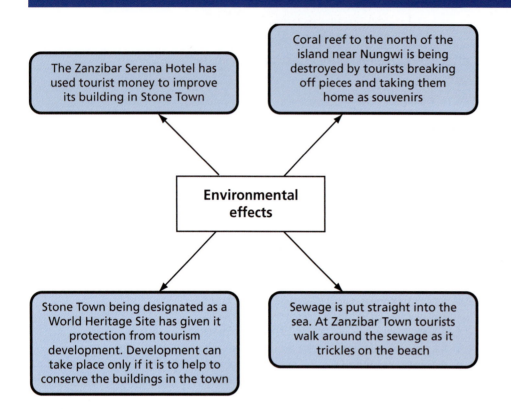

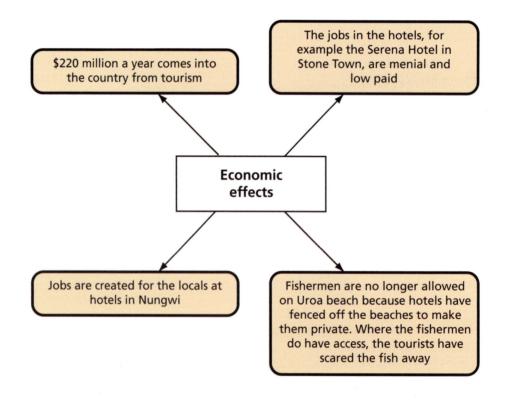

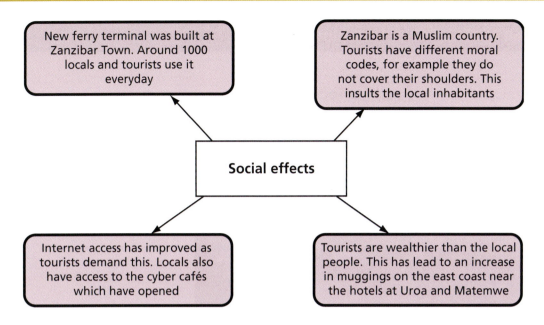

The effects of tourism on Machu Picchu

Negative	Impact	Positive
• The hotels such as the Sanctuary Lodge at Machu Picchu is owned by Orient-Express Hotels group. Therefore, much of the profit made from tourism leaves the country. • The high-paying jobs are done by foreigners not local people, who are brought in to work by the foreign hotel company.	Economic	• Tourists spend money in the area, such as on handicrafts at the local market in Pisac. • Machu Picchu generates $40 million a year in income for the Peruvian government.
• Garbage is thrown into the Urubamba River. • Erosion is occurring on the Inca Trail due to the pressure of tourists. In 1998, 53,500 tourists walked the trail.	Environmental	• The tourists pay $50 each to travel the Inca Trail. • Machu Picchu has been designated a World Heritage Site to protect it from large numbers of tourists.
• The local villagers who are employed as porters, are made to carry bags weighing up to 50 kg. • The local villagers are affected by the clothes of the Western visitors and wish to dress like them.	Social	• Porters since 2000 have been limited to carrying a load of 25 kg. • Tourism provides jobs and opportunities to sell souvenirs this has improved the standard of living for the local people.

ACTIVITY

Study photographs A and B on page 53. Explain the effects of tourism on the areas in the photograph. Try to mention a social, economic and environmental effect both positive and negative.

Exam Tip

- You could be asked questions that require recall of knowledge.
- You should learn at least one specific social, economic and environmental effect both positive and negative.
- You may be asked questions about the effects of tourism on a photograph of an area you don't know. In this case you will have to apply your knowledge about general effects to the area shown.

Unit 3 The Human Environment

The effects of tourism on Malham in the Yorkshire Dales

Social effects

The National Trust runs a shuttle bus service from Settle to Malham on weekends and Bank Holidays throughout the summer. It costs £2 return. It runs every hour from 10.30 a.m. until 4.30 p.m.

The local shop stays open all week in the summer due to the trade from tourists. In the winter it is only open 3 days a week.

There are a large number of billboards, such as the Yorkshire Dales pony trekking centre board. This is displayed in the main street even though the National Park authority has banned them because they ruin the authenticity of the village.

Visitors tend to park in the narrow village streets causing congestion. The local residents are prevented from going about their necessary activities and access for emergency vehicles is severely restricted.

Economic effects

The farmer at Town Head Farm has opened a campsite charging £10 a night per tent.

Over 55% of the houses in Malham are used for holiday purposes. This makes it very difficult for the locals, especially young couples, to buy property in the area.

There are also numerous cafés and shops in the village which cater for the tourists, such as The Cove Centre. These provide employment opportunities for the local people.

Tourism provides new jobs such as a waitress at The Barn tea shop; the employment is, however, seasonal and poorly paid.

Chapter 6 A Tourist's World

Environmental effects

Eroded paths have been restored in the Goredale area with money raised from the car park fees.

The Malham area is very popular with approximately 100,000 visits per year. This causes erosion of footpaths, especially the footpath to Janet's Foss waterfall which is one of the closest attractions to the village.

Malham is in the Yorkshire Dales National Park. This means that it is protected by the laws of the Park which restrict development that is not in keeping with the natural environment. For example, any new houses have to be built using local stone.

Tourists walk over the land of the farmer at Town Head Farm when they walk to Malham Cove. They leave gates open and visitors' dogs disturb animals.

ACTIVITIES

Study the effects of tourism on the four tourist destinations. Take each destination in turn:
- Describe and explain: one social, one economic and one environmental effect of tourism.
- Remember to include specific points (examples).

Exam Tip

For questions that ask for examples, your answer will be marked as follows:

Foundation Tier
Each point will receive a mark. If your answer does not contain a specific point about an example you will lose one mark.

Higher Tier
If the command word is **outline** or **describe**, these questions will usually be marked out of four marks. Each point will receive a mark. If your answer does not include specific points about an example you will only receive two marks. If examples are asked for and you only give one, you will lose one mark.

Exam Tip

- You may be asked to describe a distribution on a map. You should start with general points.
- Your answer should then become more specific.
- If data is asked for, you will lose a mark if you don't include it.
- If data is not requested you should still include some as you will be given credit.

Unit 3 The Human Environment

Ecotourism

Ecotourism

Sustainable tourism is 'tourism which leads to the management of all resources in such a way that economic, social and aesthetic needs can be fulfilled while maintaining cultural integrity, essential ecological processes, biological diversity and life support systems.'

In more simple terms this means that sustainable tourism is a process which meets the needs of present tourists and host communities while protecting and enhancing the needs of future generations.

Ecotourism: a branch of sustainable tourism. Ecotourism is responsible travel to natural areas that conserves the environment and improves the well-being of local people

The principles of ecotourism

'Footsteps' is an ecotourism destination in The Gambia. It is built in the style of a traditional African village compound, with nine accommodation huts. It is located close to the village of Gunjur and is open all year round. Most of the tourists come from the UK. The green boxes opposite describe how it protects the environment; the purple boxes describe how it benefits the local community.

ACTIVITY

Explain the reasons why Footsteps is an example of an ecotourist destination.

Exam Tip

Case study questions will use the following mark scheme:

Foundation Tier

Level 1 (1–2) A simple answer which has very little description. Could be about anywhere, not linked to any particular study.
Level 2 (3–4) A basic answer with level two being reached by there being descriptive points or a specific point or possibly a weak explanation. The top of the level requires a specific point and some linked descriptive points or a specific point and weak explanation.
Level 3 (5–6) A clear answer with level three being reached by there being a clear explanation or a specific point. The top of the level requires a range of specific points or a number of explanations or a specific point and an explanation.

Higher Tier

Level 1 (1–2) A basic answer which has simple descriptive statements.
Level 2 (3–4) A clear answer with level two being reached by there being an explanation or a specific point. The top of the level requires a range of specific points or a number of explanations or a specific point and an explanation.
Level 3 (5–6) An explicit answer with a range of specific and explained points.

Chapter 6 A Tourist's World

Footsteps has its own vegetable gardens which provide everything the tourists need. There are also fruit trees (banana, mango, orange) which grow around the huts.

Ducks are kept which provide eggs. Footsteps tries to be as self-sufficient as possible.

The huts are made from local wood and materials. The furniture is made by craftsmen from Gunjur from local wood.

Electricity is produced using the wind and the sun. The solar-powered freezer has considerably reduced the use of propane gas.

Footsteps gives 20% of its profit to the local community.

The water for the swimming pool is filtered through reed beds to get rid of impurities.

There is a shop at Footsteps which sells 'tie dye' and Batik work which is made on site by local women. Footsteps also has information for their guests about local markets and craftsmen.

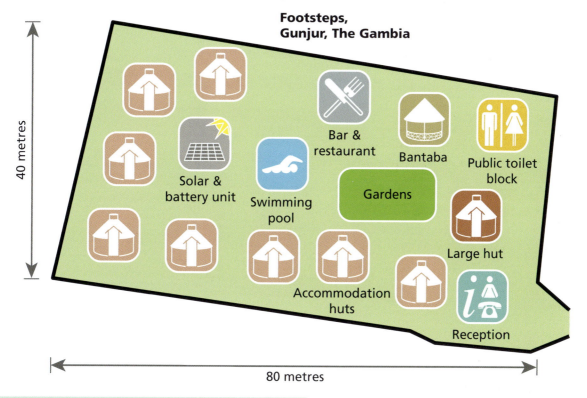

Footsteps, Gunjur, The Gambia

All the toilets at Footsteps Eco Lodge are composting toilets. This means that all harmful substances are removed, which allows the waste to be used as compost.

Footsteps employs all 22 of its staff from the local village of Gunjur. The employees receive training and are paid for all of the year, unlike most locally employed staff who are laid off out of season. They get medical and dental care.

Water is very scarce. The water for the huts comes from tube wells and is stored in water tanks. Solar-powered pumps are used to fill up the water tanks. The water which has been used by guests in sinks, baths and for washing clothes, is known as grey water. It is filtered and then used to irrigate the fruit and vegetables grown in the gardens.